TWENTIETH CENTURY INTERPRETATIONS
OF

THE

PARDONER'S

TALE

A Collection of Critical Essays

Edited by

DEWEY R. FAULKNER

Prentice-Hall, Inc. A SPECTRUM BOOK *Englewood Cliffs, N.J.*

Library of Congress Cataloging in Publication Data

FAULKNER, DEWEY R.   comp.
    Twentieth century interpretations of the Pardoner's tale.

    (A Spectrum Book)
    Bibliography: p.
    1. Chaucer, Geoffrey, d. 1400. Canterbury tales.
Pardoner's tale. I. Title.
PR1868.P3F3   821'.1   73-9998
ISBN 0-13-648758-0
ISBN 0-13-648741-6 (pbk.)

10 9 8 7 6 5 4 3 2 1

PRENTICE-HALL INTERNATIONAL, INC. (*London*)
PRENTICE-HALL OF AUSTRALIA, PTY. LTD. (*Sydney*)
PRENTICE-HALL OF CANADA, LTD. (*Toronto*)
PRENTICE-HALL OF INDIA PRIVATE LIMITED (*New Delhi*)
PRENTICE-HALL OF JAPAN, INC. (*Tokyo*)

Contents

Introduction

by Dewey R. Faulkner

In a sense, the fourteenth century began and ended with a pardoner. Chaucer created his character, one of the century's most vivid fictional personalities, in its last decade. The earlier pardoner was a real person: Pope Boniface VIII celebrated the Church's first Jubilee Year in 1300 by granting indulgences, or pardons, on a grand scale.

> To Romans who, within the space of that year, visited the churches of the Blessed Apostles St. Peter and St. Paul for thirty consecutive days, and to all others who were not Romans who did so for fifteen days, a full and complete pardon of all sins would be granted as well as remission of guilt and punishment [di colpa e di pena], provided the sins were or would be confessed.[1]

These two figures are alike in being extraordinarily evil. Boniface finds a literary niche in Dante's *Commedia*, which is set in early April of the Jubilee Year, where St. Peter calls him "That one who on earth/ usurps my place, my place which is vacant/ in the sight of the Son of God,/ [who] has made of my cemetery a sewer/ of blood and filth, so that the perverse one [Lucifer]/ who fell from here is pleased" (*Paradiso* XXVII. 22–27).[2] Chaucer's Pardoner cannot make such claims for himself; he is a petty operator by comparison to the Pope. On closer inspection, however, he will be seen to be far more dangerous than Boniface; he is certainly far more evil.

The Pardoner's occupation is his name, and the reverse is also true. Since the office of pardoner, or *quaestor,* is now extinct, it will be worthwhile to review what his occupation involved. The best discussion of this is Professor Donaldson's:

> The medieval pardoner's function was to collect money for charitable enterprises supported by branches of the church and to act as the Pope's agent in rewarding donors with some temporal remission of their sins. According to theological doctrine, St. Peter—and through him his papal

---

[1] Villani, *Chronicle,* trans. Charles S. Singleton, in *Dante Aligheri: The Divine Comedy: Inferno, Vol. 2: Commentary* (Princeton: Princeton University Press, 1970), p. 315.
[2] All quotations from Dante are from *Dante Aligheri: The Divine Comedy,* trans. H. R. Huse (New York: Holt, Rinehart and Winston, 1954).

successors—received from Christ the power to make a gift of mercy
from God's infinite treasury to those of the faithful that had earned
special favor, such as contributors to charity. The charitable enterprises
themselves—generally hospitals—hired pardoners to raise money, but
the pardoners had also to be licensed by the Pope to pass on to contributors the papal indulgence. By canon law pardoners were permitted
to work only in a prescribed area; within that area they might visit
churches during Sunday service, briefly explain their mission, receive
contributions, and, in the Pope's name, issue indulgence, which was
considered not a sale, but a free gift made in return for a free gift. In
actual fact pardoners seem seldom to have behaved as the law required
them. Since a parish priest was forbidden to exclude properly licensed
pardoners, they made their way into churches at will, and once there
did not confine themselves to a mere statement of their business, but
rather, in order to make the congregation free of its gifts, preached
highly emotive sermons and boasted of the extraordinary efficacy of their
own particular pardon, claiming for it powers that not even the Pope
could have invested it with. An honest pardoner, if such existed, was
entitled to a percentage of his collections; dishonest pardoners took
more than their share; indeed, some were complete frauds, bearing
forged credentials which, in an age when even clerical illiteracy was
common, were no less impressive than if they had been real.[3]

Chaucer's is a "gentil PARDONER/ Of Rouncivale" (I.669–70);[4] that is,
he is based at the Hospital and Chapel of Saint Mary Roncevall at
Charing, just west of the city of London. This particular convent was
quite notorious: its buildings and lands were seized by King Richard
II in 1379 because of abuses in alms-collecting; they were restored in
1383, but in 1387 another scandal, this time involving unauthorized
sales of pardons, brought the convent again to the attention of Londoners. Finally, a flood of pardons was authorized by Pope Boniface IX
for his Jubilee Year in 1390 and the years following;[5] and "Rouncivale"
was doubtless a fountainhead for sales of these during the decade in
which Chaucer is thought to have created his member of the species.

Pardoners were regarded in their own time as far more serious spiritual threats than the above facts by themselves would indicate. The
Oxford Petition of 1414 gives the following grievances against them:

[3] E. Talbot Donaldson, *The Norton Anthology of English Literature: Revised*,
M. H. Abrams, General Editor (New York, 1968), I, 159. Reprinted by permission
of W. W. Norton & Company, Inc. Copyright © 1968, 1962 by W. W. Norton &
Company, Inc.

[4] All textual references throughout this anthology are to *The Works of Geoffrey
Chaucer: Second Edition*, ed. F. N. Robinson, New Cambridge Edition (Boston:
Houghton Mifflin Company, 1957). In general, references to lines in fragment VI
(Physician's and Pardoner's tales) are given without the fragment number through-
out; references to other tales include the Roman numeral.

[5] See John Matthews Manly, *Some New Light on Chaucer* (New York: H. Holt &
Co., 1926), pp. 127–28; and Muriel Bowden, *A Commentary on the General Prologue
to the Canterbury Tales* (New York: The Macmillan Company, 1962), pp. 284–86.

Although not in holy orders, they preach publicly, and pretend falsely that they have full powers of absolving both living and dead alike from punishment and guilt, along with other blasphemies, by means of which they plunder and seduce the people, and in all probability drag them down with their own person to the infernal regions, by affording them frivolous hope and an audacity to commit sin.[6]

Their ability to damn souls is especially important in Chaucer's tale; it is an ability common to pardoner and Pope. Boniface VIII, for example, has dragged (or sent) Guido da Montefeltro to the infernal regions by saying, "Do not let your heart mistrust,/ right now I absolve you" (*Inferno* XXVII.100–101), parodying Christ's "Let not your heart be troubled, neither let it be afraid," and "my peace I give unto you" (John 14 : 27).

This common ability and the common parodic techniques used to portray it (Chaucer's use of this technique will be frequently discussed in this volume) may indicate a connection between Chaucer and Dante that is more than simple coincidence. Chaucer knew the *Commedia* well by the 1390s and may even have had a manuscript of the poem with him on his return in May, 1373, from his first Italian journey, to Genoa and Florence. Imitations of passages in Dante appear first in *The House of Fame*, most probably composed only after Chaucer's second Italian journey, in 1378. Prior to this, Chaucer's poetic interests centered on translating and imitating fashionable French poets: Guillaume de Lorris, Machaut, Deschamps, and others. *The House of Fame* and its successor, *The Parliament of Fowls*, introduced new Italian elements into what remain recognizably French forms; but Chaucer soon met the Italians on their own—and his—terms. During the later 1380s he translated, or, more precisely, recreated long Italian poems and a Latin prose work by Boccaccio and Petrarch: *Troilus and Criseyde* and the tales later given to the Knight and the Clerk. But Dante, except for scattered passages, was left alone, although not forgotten. At the end of *Troilus*, Chaucer began his *envoy* with,

> Go, litel bok, go, litel myn tragedye,
> Ther God thi makere yet, er that he dye,
> So sende myght to make in som comedye!
> (V.1786–88)

Comedy here probably is meant in the generalized medieval sense of an "imitation of life, a mirror of custom, and an image of truth";[7] but it may well also refer specifically to Dante's great *Commedia*, thus reflecting Chaucer's desire to produce his own "comedye" worthy of ri-

---

[6] Quoted in Bowden, p. 281.

[7] Translated in James I. Wimsatt, *Allegory and Mirror: Tradition and Structure in Middle English Literature* (New York: Pegasus, 1970), p. 28.

valing the Italian one. The *Canterbury Tales,* which was produced on
the whole after *Troilus,* is, in a fundamental sense, Chaucer's own answer to his prayer. Death prevented him from completing his grand
scheme, but elements of it are conspicuous in the fragments of the *Tales*
that we possess.[8] To begin, Chaucer makes his work obviously comple-
mentary to Dante's: he locates it in the one region Dante directly omits,
the everyday world; and instead of involving his native land by alluding to it, as Dante does, he places his figures in that landscape and has
them riding through it. Instead of one poet figure and various guides
meeting and interviewing persons fixed in their locales, Chaucer has
the poet and his guide (the Host) accompanied by his persons, who
volunteer their own information en route. In this case, however,
Chaucer has it both ways: the characters are also fixed in place in the
General Prologue, and the reader is given a preliminary guided tour
of them there by the poet.

It is the revelatory monologue, beyond these, that connects the two
poems most closely: it is, I think, as valid to speak of 'Francesca's Tale,'
'Ulysses' Tale,' and 'Ugolino's Tale' as to speak of the 'Wife of Bath's
Tale,' the 'Merchant's Tale,' and the 'Pardoner's Tale.' Chaucer need
not have taken over the device from Dante, but he does use it much
as the Italian poet does. Both the Chaucerian and Dantean characters
mentioned use their tales, or narratives, as *exempla* for positions that
they wish to present, or for ideas that they wish to sell; and they all
try to focus our attention on themselves—but not too closely, of course,
lest we see too much of their true nature. We observe and sympathize
with their human woes, both in life and in hell; but we are compelled,
frequently by that same image which evokes our greatest sympathy
(such as Ugolino's 'just revenge' in gnawing Ruggiero's head images his
plight in being forced to devour his children) to evaluate them *sub
specie aeternitatis* (the gnawing images Ugolino devouring his homeland, the real reason for his damnation). In the character of the Pardoner—and it is the narrator that is our real interest here—Chaucer
pushes this technique to its furthest limits in the *Canterbury Tales.*
The poet focuses our attention on two aspects of his creation's character to make his points: the Pardoner's lack of an essential quality,
and the irreconcilable duality basic to his nature, a duality that frequently appears as an ambiguity at crucial places in his monologue.

Chaucer prepares us for these aspects long before the Pardoner's tale
proper. In the *General Prologue* the Pardoner is placed at the end of
the list of pilgrims, putting him directly opposite the virtuous Knight
and thus making him morally suspect. Moreover, he is imaged as an
animal, something subhuman: he is shown singing love songs with his

---

[8] See the discussion of Chaucer's moral and structural intent in Robert O. Payne,
The Key of Remembrance (New Haven and London: Yale University Press, 1963),
pp. 147–70.

friend the Summoner in a voice "as smal as hath a goot" (668), and has
eyes "glarynge . . . as an hare" (684), no beard, and long, thin, yellow
locks, characteristics which indicated malice, deceptiveness, and effeminacy to the medieval audience.[9] The animal similes give way to meta-
phoric identification in the clinching line, "I trow he were a geldyng
or a mare" (691). The Pardoner admits to practicing duplicity: he has
numerous relics with which he deceives and robs the poor (694–706);
and he sings and preaches well in church—he is a "noble ecclesiaste"
(708)—but does so only "To wynne silver, as he ful wel coude" (713).
After the *General Prologue* we see him once again, interrupting the
Wife of Bath's 'sermon' to announce that "I was aboute to wedde a
wyf; allas!" (III.166). This is rather a surprising statement for a "geldyng
or a mare" and presumably represents an attempt by the Pardoner to
forestall the issue of his effeminacy. It is to no avail: the Host touches
on it by calling him "beel amy" (VI.318) before the Pardoner's speech.
There are other privations, but this one gives Chaucer his physical
symbol and prepares us for the later spiritual ones.

We are prepared for the more serious levels of the *Pardoner's Tale*
through the sequence of tales that precede it. It is found nearly always
following the *Physician's Tale* in fragment VI, which, in the Ellsmere
and related manuscripts, in turn follows the *Franklin's Tale* and the
remainder of fragments III, IV, and V. The resulting order of tales
is as follows: Wife of Bath—Friar—Summoner—Clerk—Merchant—
Squire—Franklin—Physician—Pardoner. Now the first tale, the Wife's,
is interrupted twice, first by the Pardoner and then by the Friar and
the Summoner. The latter two are immediately at each other's throats
following the conclusion of the Wife's tale, much as they were when
they interrupted her earlier. The Pardoner, however, waits until last
and aims at all the pilgrims.[10]

The Wife, Clerk, Merchant, and Franklin are normally associated
in a continuing discussion generally referred to as the 'marriage group,'
even though marriage is only one of a complex of topics discussed.
The Franklin brings his tale to a happy conclusion which, for himself
and for many critics, ends the discussion of marriage happily as well.
This happy ending comes about, however, because of the Franklin's
views on evil in mankind, views that neither the Physician nor the
Pardoner allow to go unchallenged.

The Physician makes his challenge by the deliberate parallels between his tale and the Franklin's.[11] Dorigen and Virginia are con-

---

[9] See Bowden, pp. 247–76.
[10] See Bernard F. Huppé, *A Reading of the Canterbury Tales* (Albany: State University of New York Press, 1964), pp. 208–9 and 218–19.
[11] Some of these parallels are discussed by Paul G. Beidler, "The Pairing of the
Franklin's Tale and the Physician's Tale," *Chaucer Review*, III (1968–69), 275–79.
My own ideas were developed before I saw Mr. Beidler's essay, the concerns of
which differ largely from mine.

trasted. Virginia, for example, "hath ful ofte tyme syk hire feyned,/ For that she wolde fleen the compaignye/ Where likely was to treten of folye,/ As is at feestes, revels, and at daunces,/ That been occasions of daliaunces" (VI.62–66); Dorigen, of course, meets Aurelius at an after-dinner revel with dancing (V.917–30), where she "in play" makes the proposition that sets up the crisis of the tale. Then too, "alle hire [Virginia's] wordes [were] Sownynge in vertu and in gentillesse" (VI. 53–54); the latter quality is the Franklin's favorite, whereas the former recalls the Clerk (cf. I.307). There are numerous other parallels in the description, upon which the Physician lavishes 117 of the 286 lines in his tale. After it concludes, he makes the plot of the tale proper also parallel to the Franklin's: in both a man and woman are united by a lawful relationship (Arveragus-Dorigen/ Virginius-Virginia) which is threatened by a lustful man (Aurelius/ Appius) who uses another man as his agent (the clerk/ Claudius) to gain the woman. In both tales the woman is forced to choose whether she will yield to the authority of her man: Dorigen and Arveragus compromise; whereas Virginia yields to her father, who sees the man's absolute authority as the only guide: "O gemme of chastitee, in pacience/ Take thou thy deeth, for this is my sentence" (VI.223–24). (There is here also a probable allusion to patient Griselda in the *Clerk's Tale*.) In the *Franklin's Tale* the com-promise works, one good deed prompts several more, mercy and for-giveness reign, and all live happily ever after. The Physician, however, will have none of this: justice, not mercy, reigns in his tale. Appius is about to have Virginius executed when "right anon a thousand peple in thraste,/ To save the knyght, for routhe and for pitee,/ For knowen was the false iniquitee" (VI.260–62); that is, the cavalry arrives. The villains are justly punished, although Claudius's sentence is reduced to exile through Virginius's "pitee" (269–73), and the Physician concludes all with his moral, "Forsaketh synne, er synne yow forsake" (286), a commonplace call to repentance (cf. the *Parson's Tale*, X.93).

Both the Franklin's and Physician's tales are based on views of evil that are only partly valid. The Franklin's view resembles that which Mrs. Shelley attributed (not quite justly) to her late husband, Percy Bysshe Shelley: "evil is not inherent in the system of the creation, but an accident that might be expelled. . . . Shelley believed that man-kind had only to will that there should be no evil, and there would be none." [12] The Physician's view is quite different. Appius sees Virginia, admires her, and "Anon the feend into his herte ran,/ And taughte hym sodeynly that he by slyghte/ The mayden to his purpos wynne myghte" (VI.130–32). The will to sin is man's, but a very real outside agent is willing to help with the means. When the Physician says that

[12] Note on *Prometheus Unbound*, in *Shelley: Poetical Works*, ed. Thomas Hutch-inson, Oxford Standard Authors (London: Oxford University Press, 1967), p. 271.

sin will forsake man, he is probably speaking of a real external force, not merely making an abstract statement. Likewise, the justice in his tale is of the *deus ex machina* variety: "Beth war, for no man woot whom God wol smyte/ In no degree" (VI.279–80). Man emerges as a pawn in a cosmic battle of good and evil: human will opens the way for the participants, the human agents conduct themselves strictly according to law, and justice finally triumphs by the sword—either 'the people's' or Virginius's. (It is ironic that Virginius shows mercy to Claudius rather than to his daughter.) The Physician's views are as grim as the Franklin's views, which he refutes, are optimistic.

The Pardoner, who has the final say on evil in this sequence, makes both views appear inadequate. The Pardoner is not about to "will that there should be no evil"; it is in fact doubtful if he could. In his tale one evil turn prompts another; and the rebirth implicit in the Franklin's Christmas scene is countered by the grove up the crooked way and the tree that brings death into the rioters' world. The Physician's devil has a counterpart in the *Pardoner's Tale* (844–48), but there is no cavalry to save the rioters. Even the devil appears as a formality, since he should appear in such places, as do Dante's devils in *Inferno* XXI–XXII. Evil in the Pardoner's tale is at once both far more complex and far simpler than it is in its two predecessors.

The tale itself is only part of a larger structure, which can be diagrammed as follows:

A. Interchange between Pardoner and Host (287–328)
B. Pardoner's speech to pilgrims (329–462)
C. Exemplum ('Tale') (462–83)
D. Denunciation of:
   1. Gluttony (Flesh) (483–588)
   2. Gambling (World) (589–628)
   3. Swearing (Devil) (629–60)
C. Exemplum ('Tale') continued (661–894)
B. Another speech to pilgrims (895–940)
A. Another interchange between Pardoner and Host (941–68)

This 'Chinese box' structure places the denunciation of sins at the center, where it belongs in a sermon, and relates the tale to it as an *exemplum*, an illustrative story designed to reinforce the sermon's theme, the text, *Radix malorum est Cupiditas—Cupiditas* is the root of all evil. As has been frequently pointed out, the three sins denounced are related to this text only if *cupiditas* is defined generally as 'love of things of this world for their own sakes, and especially love of self.' [13] The Pardoner, however, defines it as "coveityse" (424, 433) and "avarice" (428), which is "that same vice/ Which that I use" (427–28). In

---

[13] See the selection by D. W. Robertson in this volume, p. 118.

the same fashion, while the three rioters in the exemplum are guilty of the three denounced 'tavern' vices, and of avarice as well, they can be indicted for numerous other vices also, thus making the exemplum fit both definitions of *cupiditas*. The Pardoner's intentions are ambiguous on this point.

Chaucer has prepared us for this kind of situation with the notorious line in the *General Prologue*, "I trow he were a geldyng or a mare" (I.691). This actually says, 'I *believe* he was either a eunuch *or* a homosexual,' although critics have been quick to seize upon one or the other possibility as a fact and use it as a psychological entrance into—or club to beat—the tale. Chaucer, however, says only 'I believe' and 'either/or.' Even so, the central point is clear enough: something that should belong to the Pardoner, his physical masculinity, is missing. Translated from physical into spiritual terms, this privation becomes symbolic of evil in the Pardoner's character:

> What is called *evil* in the substance of a thing is only a lack of some quality which ought naturally to be there. . . . Now the term *privation*, considered strictly and in its proper sense, designates the absence or want of what a being ought naturally to possess. It is to privation of this kind that evil is limited. Evil is a pure negation within a substance. It is not an essence, not a reality.[14]

The exact nature of the privation is ambiguous; and although Chaucer is inexplicit about its existence ("I trow"), the Pardoner's very eagerness to hide it makes us all the more certain of its existence and importance.

The physical lack, however, is not the most important of the Pardoner's privations. He clearly thinks he lacks the goods of this world and expends all his energies to obtain them: "moneie, wolle, chese, and whete . . . licour of the vyne,/ And . . . a joly wenche in every toun" (448–53). But his true lack is one of concern for the souls of those with whom he deals; the Pardoner mentions this and passes on, but the situation registers because of the curious image he uses:

> I rekke nevere, whan that they been beryed,
> Though that hir soules goon a-blakeberyed!
>
> (405–6)

Christ Himself has warned against just this man: "fear him which is able to destroy both soul and body in hell" (Matthew 10 : 28); and, not surprisingly, the Pardoner prefers to spend most of his time detailing only his methods for despoiling his audiences of their physical pos-

14 Etienne Gilson, *The Christian Philosophy of St. Thomas Aquinas* (New York: Random House, 1956), p. 156. Cf. St. Thomas Aquinas, *Summa Contra Gentiles*, III, ch. 7.

sessions, their bodies. His motive, malignancy or indifference, is ambiguous; his effect, the destruction of the soul, is not.

It should also be noted here that the Pardoner is not so totally honest in exposing himself as at first it might seem. He allows his claims for his pardons' efficacy to stand (cf. 906–915), especially that for absolution from the sin itself (pardon *a culpa*); real pardons are intended only to lessen the penance for the sin (pardon *a poena*), making this claim especially dangerous for the buyer. Likewise, the messy business of repenting before one can have pardon "Al newe and fressh at every miles ende" (928) is never mentioned. Perhaps the light tone of this passage (904–945) invalidates this objection; yet the Pardoner, offering to the Host, clearly seems to hope that it will not. A serious offer and a joking tone: they do not fuse in the Pardoner's mouth, although the Host's serious refusal of the offer combines in his mouth with a jesting tone, as we shall see.

This peculiar inability to reconcile elements which are merely juxtaposed in his character is, like privation, one of the Pardoner's connections with the medieval concepts of evil. The privation here is unity. By definition, only God is absolutely good and absolutely one; all else is deficient in goodness and unity. Physically, for example, man's division into two sexes is a deficiency, even though it is a divinely created situation and therefore good. Still, unity is to be preferred, and it can be found spiritually in the Church: "There is neither Jew nor Greek, there is neither bond nor free, there is neither male nor female: for ye are all one in Jesus Christ" (Galatians 3 : 28). The Pardoner, "neither male nor female," is a parody of this state of unity.

Far more important is Ephesians 2 : 14–16: "For he [Christ] is our peace, who hath made [the two] [15] one, and hath broken down the middle wall of partition between us; . . . for to make in himself of twain one new man, so making peace; And that he might reconcile both unto God in one body by the cross, having slain the enmity thereby." The Pardoner's "middle wall of partition" is intact; the twain in him remain resolutely separate. His tale is about the Old Man, not the New Man. Like Spenser's Duessa, he is "the two" and, as such, is fundamentally a symbol of pure evil.

It can, of course, be argued that the Pardoner is less a symbol than a human being, primarily because there is some good in him. This is to an extent true, but the good in the Pardoner is of special kinds. He himself admits to one kind in two places:

[15] The King James' "both" obscures the meaning of both the original and the Vulgate (*utraque*), and I have corrected accordingly. The passage is remarkably similar to logion 22 of the Gnostic *Gospel of Thomas*. On the question of divine unity opposed to the duality of evil, see Mircea Eliade, *The Two and the One*, trans. J. M. Cohen (New York: Harper & Row, 1965), pp. 103–7.

> But though myself be gilty in that synne,
> Yet kan I maken oother folk to twynne
> From avarice, and soore to repente.
>
>   (429–31)

> For though myself be a ful vicious man,
> A moral tale yet I yow telle kan.
>
>   (459–60)

This is not a good *in* the Pardoner, however, but rather a good use to which he can be put by a higher power. His more usual way of incorporating good is by parodying it:

> Youre names I entre heer in my rolle anon;
> Into the blisse of hevene shul ye gon.
> I yow assoile, by myn heigh power,
> Yow that wol offre, as clene and eek as cleer
> As ye were born. . . .   (911–15)

"My rolle" is the Pardoner's version of the Book of Life at the Apocalypse: "And I saw the dead, small and great, stand before God; and the books were opened; and another book was opened, which is the book of life; and the dead were judged out of those things which were written in the books, according to their works" (Revelation 20 : 12). Similarly, the Pardoner's promise to "assoile" men "as clene and eek as cleer as ye were born" is derived from Christ's "Except a man be born again, he cannot see the kingdom of God" (John 3 : 3). In both these parodies the Pardoner is identifying himself with Christ and usurping His prerogatives; he is beginning to assume the form of antichrist but withdraws at the last minute into himself: "And lo, sires, thus I preche" (915). Even Dante would, I think, envy the brilliance with which Chaucer handles his character here.

There remains the most notorious of the Pardoner's good or virtuous passages:

> And Jhesu Crist, that is oure soules leche,
> So graunte yow his pardoun to receyve,
> For that is best; I wol yow nat deceyve.
>
>   (916–18)

This simply sits in the tale, unconnected to its surroundings; and there is a reason for this, one not associated with the Pardoner's psychology but again, I think, closely related to medieval thought on evil:

> The relation between evil and the good which supports it is never such that evil can consume or, as it were, totally exhaust the good. Could it do so, evil would consume and totally exhaust even itself. So long,

indeed, as evil subsists, it must have a subject in which to subsist. Now the subject of evil is the good. Hence there always remains some good.[16]

The Pardoner exists, therefore he cannot be totally evil, therefore some good must be in him, and in lines 916–18, pure and untainted, there it is.

This passage, the parodies of Christ, and the Pardoner's joking dishonesties all fall within the second *B* passage (895–940) in my diagram; it is here that the Pardoner's true nature, the paradigm of evil, manifests itself. From 895 to 945 the good precipitates out, while the Pardoner's evil techniques and themes are combined more elaborately than before: everything we must know about the Pardoner is contained in these lines, either directly or allusively.

The Pardoner's attack on the Host (941–57) is something of a return to psychological realism. The Pardoner is motivated: the Host "Hath trespassed . . . to me" (416) with his veiled reference to the Pardoner's effeminacy before the tale began (318). The Pardoner may even be drunk and not aware of what he is saying (cf. 321–22, 327–28, and 426); as he himself has said,

> . . . dronkenesse is verray sepulture
> Of mannes wit and his discrecioun.
> In whom that drynke hath dominacioun
> He kan no conseil kepe, it is no drede.
>
> (558–61)

At the same time, the situation has a symbolic function of some importance. The Host's response, "thanne have I Cristes curs!" is as ambiguous as anything the Pardoner has said. It can mean either 'even if I should have Christ's curse,' or 'then I shall have Christ's curse (if I accept your relics)'; and in either interpretation it reflects one of the possible valid responses to the Pardoner. The Host then proceeds to imitate the Pardoner's parodies of holy things (951–55)—he clearly does not think the Pardoner a eunuch, by the way—and in so doing reduces the Pardoner to infuriated silence. Thus the Pardoner, for whom the perverted word derived from true Word, Christ, is a means to gain things, loses his one agency of potency: "This Pardoner answerde nat a word;/ So wrooth he was, no word ne wolde he seye" (956–57). The sin of avarice is overcome by the sin of wrath: "And if Satan rise up against himself, and be divided, he cannot stand, but hath an end" (John 3 : 26). In the Pardoner, contradictions do not ultimately resolve in paradox; they cancel each other out, leaving only the highly ambiguous kiss at the end (968).

[16] Gilson, p. 157.

These contradictions in the Pardoner extend to his *exemplum* or tale as well, and especially apply to the strange Old Man in it. The facts about this character are not puzzling: he is old and poor; he greets the three rioters "ful mekely" and piously (714–15); he is described as completely covered, even shrouded, except for his face (717); he tells the three that he can find no young man (which they are) to exchange his youth for his age, implying that this is the condition for his much-desired death; he knocks with his staff upon the earth, his mother, asking to be let in, offering to change his "cheste" for a hairshirt, which is normally associated with penance (734–36); he admonishes the young men to honor him and let him pass, dismissing them with "God be with yow, where ye go or ryde" (748); the rioters threaten him, asking where death is to be found, and calling him "oon of his [Death's] assent/ To sleen us yonge folk" (758–59); the Old Man informs them that Death is up "this croked wey," in a "grove," under an oak; he again dismisses them piously, if more sharply: "God save yow, that boghte agayn mankynde,/ And yow amende!" (766–67). The rioters find Death—or rather the gold that produces the cupidity in them that causes Death—in the roots of the oak, *radix malorum* indeed.

The Old Man is thus, presumably, not Death himself. Allegorical representations of death, as in the *Castle of Perseverance* and the various pictorial Dances of Death, usually have the character identify himself verbally and show him with his skull face and dart or spear. Indeed, the Old Man is most kind, patient, and pious toward the young rioters, so much so that several recent interpreters have found him to be God's agent, offering God's mercy to the erring rioters, who are symbolic of mankind.[17] This is somewhat excessive, I think, since the Old Man merely gives the rioters a lecture in deportment, in which he paraphrases Christ's Golden Rule. Furthermore, he does not directly send the young men to their deaths: he simply tells them where some gold is, thereby doing them a favor.

On the other hand, the Old Man does seem to know what will happen to the young men when they find this gold, much as the Pardoner knows his audience's weaknesses. And his affinities with the Wandering Jew would indicate that, like the Jew, he is being forced to wander eternally for having offended God grievously in some way. He wishes, for some reason, to have a penitential "heyre clowt," for which he will exchange his "cheste." Robinson assures us that this is a clothes chest and not a coffin, but the word has the latter meaning at least twice earlier in this sequence of tales.[18] A coffin would be a suitable possession

---

[17] See Christopher Dean, "Salvation, Damnation and the Role of the Old Man in the *Pardoner's Tale*," *Chaucer Review*, III (1968–69), 44–49; and cf. the Steadman essay in this collection.

[18] Editorial note to l. 734, p. 751; cf. III.502 and IV.29.

for him; and to exchange it for an agent of further penance would indicate his humility. But then, it could be a money chest, filled with florins which he has been hoarding: such is the frequent attribute of avarice in medieval depictions, the sin itself being commonly represented by an old man.[19] His ironic gift of florins to the rioters would then, appropriately, be a parody of the virtue opposed to avarice, Largesse, which is frequently shown giving money away.[20] No one interpretation incorporates all the details, most of which, one suspects, Chaucer has introduced to make him both ambiguous and contradictory, reflecting the Pardoner.

We cannot accept such a situation, of course, and we thus return repeatedly to the Old Man and his creator, the Pardoner, hoping to make him work better this time somehow. In so doing, especially if we read the tale aloud, as was presumably Chaucer's intent, we recreate the Pardoner within ourselves for the duration of our reading; and we recognize, moreover, the elements which are common to ourselves and him. What we do about the failings of our moral natures thus exposed is very much our decision. Unlike Dante, who presents himself in the poem as an exemplary personality developing positively through interaction with the various figures he encounters on his journey, Chaucer merely asks us to take the journey with him and to become engaged personally, as well as intellectually, with his pilgrim figures. The Host offers some exemplary responses; but ours—as will be seen from the varied essays in this collection—are entirely up to us.

Chaucer's treatment of the Pardoner is the exact opposite of that given the other great personality in the *Canterbury Tales,* the Wife of Bath. She begins as a walking antifeminist joke (husbands 1–3) and develops into a recognizably human figure (husbands 4–5).[21] The Pardoner, on the other hand, begins as a human being and reveals himself progressively to be an inhuman thing, the image of vice as it acts on the body and the soul and, at the same time, the image of the soul which vice has consumed. He lacks the grandeur of the great evil figures; Boniface VIII would have sneered at him. But it is because of this ability to appear so petty, so eminently ignorable, that the Pardoner is most dangerous, perhaps more dangerous than the Pope. He is the 'uncreating word' made flesh, dwelling within us as well as among us; he is at once *multum in parvo* and *parvum in multo.* In the words

---

[19] A splendid illuminated illustration of this is in Rosemond Tuve's *Allegorical Imagery* (Princeton: Princeton University Press, 1966), p. 100.

[20] See Samuel C. Chew, *The Pilgrimage of Life* (New Haven and London: Yale University Press, 1962), pp. 106–7, 130–31, and 353.

[21] The parallel is emphasized by parallel statements of the two characters: the Wife's, "For myn entente is nat but for to pleye" (III.192), is echoed in the Pardoner's "For myn entente is nat but for to wynne" (VI.403).

of a most perceptive nineteenth-century interpreter, he has been well described as

> the Age's Knave, who always commands and domineers over the high and low vulgar. This man is sent in every age for a rod and a scourge, and for a blight, for a trial of men, to divide the classes of men; he is in the most holy sanctuary, and he is suffered by Providence for wise ends, and has also his great use, and his grand leading destiny.[22]

[22] William Blake, "Descriptive Catalogue" in *Blake: Complete Writings,* ed. Geoffrey Keynes, Oxford Standard Authors (London: Oxford University Press, 1966), p. 570.

PART ONE

Interpretations

The Pardoner's Confession

by Bertrand H. Bronson

In discussing the fitness of . . . tales to their tellers, we must be chary of deducing the poet's purpose from a modern effect that looms large because of contemporary preoccupations. There is testimony to the depth of Chaucer's reading of human nature when we find it not inconsistent with our latest "discoveries"; but the demonstration of such truths need not have formed any part of his deliberate intention. Thus, today, the Wife of Bath's Tale seems patently the satisfying in fantasy of her longing to recapture youth and beauty; but we can hardly assume that Chaucer set out to demonstrate the mechanism of wish-ful- ?
filment. The Märchen had a foregone conclusion as it came to him; *
and it was doubtless sufficient that it perfectly exemplified the Wife's thesis that husbands should yield sovereignty to their wives. And what, we may ask, without other clues than those provided, are we supposed to infer about the tellers' character from the Man of Law's, the Physician's, or the Manciple's tales? We are perhaps goaded to excogitate a theory only because the stories seem at first reading so *un*suitable. It might be charged that the Monk was in the same case, unless we are willing to grant that the explicit context sufficiently justified our claim that the comical inappropriateness is contributory to a deeper propriety. For here, as we have seen, *outward* circumstances already divulged, rather than an anachronistic hypothesis, prompted the explanation put forward.

Even more insidiously provocative are the self-disclosures of some other pilgrims. Notorious among these is of course the Pardoner, and of all the explanations of his "cynical avowel" Kittredge's stands preeminent for eloquence and subtlety. By virtue of the anticipatory protests of the gentlefolk lest the Pardoner tell of "ribaudye," the self-revelation, thinks Kittredge, becomes dramatically inevitable. "He is simply forestalling the reflections of his fellow-pilgrims. 'I know I am a rascal,' he says in effect, 'and *you* know it; and I wish to show you that I know you know it' . . . this time no deception is possible, and he scorns the role of a futile hypocrite." [1] Repeating a sermon to show his skill, he is carried by the momentum of his routine past the point where he ought in the present circumstances to have stopped, and adds the exhortation to take advantage of his relics and his absolution. Under the spell of his own eloquence, Kittredge believes, he is seized with a "paroxysm of agonized sincerity" that immediately gives way to wild mockery. The moment of paroxysm is signalized by three and a half lines that break—or seem to break—the tenor of discourse:

> And lo, sires, thus I preche.
> And Jhesu Crist, that is oure soules leche,
> So graunte yow his pardoun to receyve,
> For that is best; I wol yow nat deceyve.
>
> (VI. 915–18)

Here, says Kittredge, "suddenly, unexpectedly, without an instant's warning, his cynicism falls away"; but he recovers at once, and goes on with his cynical invitation to the pilgrims themselves to make offering to the relics he has just exposed as frauds.

More recently, Professor G. H. Gerould—throwing off *en passant* the delectable conjecture that the ale-stake at which the Pardoner paused for drink and a bite of bread was none other than his boon companion the Summoner, bearing in front of him his "edible buckler" and crowned with a garland "as great as it were for an ale-stake"—proceeds to interpret the whole performance of the Pardoner as that of a man who was drunk to the point of reckless garrulity. "Swept along on the tide of his own drunken eloquence . . . it is hard to say to what extent the Pardoner is conscious of what he is doing. Between ale and histrionism he is almost a somnambulist." [2] Pursuing this idea of inebriation, Gerould traces the spoor with assured skill through all the windings and rambling indirections of the Pardoner's discourse to the point where the "moral tale" truly begins, with the entrance of the three rioters on the scene. "Drink," he writes, "has not only loosened his tongue . . . but it has thoroughly befuddled him" and on this foundation his self-incrimination can be understood. But when he reached the tale, according to Gerould, Chaucer "sacrificed dramatic propriety" by taking over, himself, "as is wholly right." The tale displays all the restraint, precision, and inexorable movement that the "scrambled tirade" preceding it so conspicuously lacked. At the end, Chaucer hands back the reins to the Pardoner, who finishes with a burst of cynical and

---

[1] G. L. Kittredge, *Chaucer and His Poetry*, 1915, p. 214.
[2] G. H. Gerould, *Chaucerian Essays*, 1952, p. 62.

impudent effrontery, but carrying "one white spot on his cloak of infamy," that moment of sincerity which we must accept because it was given him by his creator, who meant him to be a human being, not a devil.

Both these theories are persuasively argued and have no small degree of dramatic appeal. Both, we should observe, rest on an assumed intention—of psychological realism—which is neither argued nor even called into question. It must be said that to make this assumption is to take for granted in Chaucer an orientation and a technical achievement that we are probably wrong in expecting before the eighteenth century, at the earliest. The episode invites our closer attention. Let us approach it this time from the rear.

After the Pardoner has completed his story, he addresses the pilgrims about him, urging them to offer good money for his absolution. "I forgot to say," he declares, "that my relics are as fine as any man's in the country, and that my pardon comes straight from the Pope's own hand. I invite any one who is moved by a spirit of devotion to come forward, kneel down, and receive absolution. Or, for a price, you can have it as you go, at frequent intervals, because one never knows what may happen, and one or other of you might fall off his horse and break his neck. You are really very lucky to have me along to assoil you in case of emergency."

Thus far, apart from his insensitive jocularity, the Pardoner might be doing business much as usual. But when he turns to the Host, we see that he is making a joke that he expects *all* the pilgrims to enjoy!

> I rede that oure Hoost heere shal bigynne,
> For he is moost envoluped in synne.
> Com forth, sire Hoost, and offre first anon,
> And thou shalt kisse the relikes everychon,
> Ye, for a grote! Unbokele anon thy purs.
>
> (VI. 941–45)

In the Pardoner's hierarchy of offenders, the worst sinner was he that kept the tightest hold on his purse-strings. Avarice was the root of all evil and the target of all the Pardoner's sermonizing; and he knew that no one could be unaware of Bailey's ruling passion. "I have an idea," Bailey had announced on the first night, "that won't cost you a thing. The one of you who tells the best stories on the way to Canterbury and back shall be given a free supper at the expense of all the rest, in this very room. And I'll even go along at my own charge, to make you the merrier and to see that you get back all right. And if any one resists my decisions, he'll have to pay scot and lot along the way." These conditions are reiterated the following morning. The point of character was clear to all of them. And in the same connection, it is unlikely that Bailey himself missed the barb aimed in his direction by the Pardoner during his mock-sermon, when the latter went out of his role to warn his imaginary country congregation against adulterated wines. "In certain places," he hints, "you order a good French wine, and when you drink it you find yourself transported to Spain." Now, Fish St. and Cheapside, as all the Pilgrims of course knew, lie just at the other end of London Bridge from where the Tabard Inn stood; and in view of this fact the reference to "othere wynes growynge faste by" is surely sufficiently pointed (VI. 566). Of course, the wine consumed on Harry Bailey's premises was a chief source of revenue to him, and to mix the cheap and cruder Spanish with the superior French was the next way to augment his profits. Few Londoners would be better informed about such doings than an experienced customs officer, which the poet happened to be.

In any case, who needed to be reminded that *Innkeeper* was a synonym for an itching palm? The Pardoner feels it a safe jibe to offer Bailey a bargain-price for his pardon: to name any sum above a groat would frighten him and defeat the man's chance of salvation. The Host's retort is indeed devastating; but I think we mistake if we attribute its grossness to violent anger. He could take the time-honoured taunt and repay it with interest. A notable thing is that he does not impugn the Pardoner's relics, but instead stigmatizes the man himself as a living lie. His contempt, not rage, is what renders the Pardoner speechless.

Now, we know that Bailey's estimate of the Pardoner is approximately correct because the Pardoner himself, in his prologue, has supplied the evidence. But, for exploratory purposes, let us suppose a stage of composition when the Pardoner's prologue did not exist. Suppose Chaucer first wrote the sermon and the tale, and stopped with the prayer quoted already, that Christ grant his own pardon to the pilgrims. This would have made an effective and appropriate conclusion, and, whatever the Pardoner's private reservations, no hypothesis would be required to explain the data in hand. Fifteen lines earlier, the Pardoner in his peroration had exclaimed:

> Allas! mankynde, how may it bitide
> That to thy creatour, which that the wroghte,
> And with his precious herte-blood thee boghte,
> Thou art so fals and so unkynde, allas?

> (VI. 900–3)

Without the prologue—which we are imagining away—the note of genuine piety would be heard in these lines. *With* the prologue, and remembering that the Pardoner's object is to get money, we may still recall that his ability to cause others to repent is something upon which he greatly values himself; and we may grant that he might hope that in the final reckoning the good so accomplished would be allowed to count however faintly in his behalf. For, although a hypocrite and a rascal, he is not an apostate. The note of sincerity in this speech is not necessarily cancelled by his vicious life. And, by the same token, he might well the more consider that true repentance would be acceptable in Heaven's eye, whether the relics that were the agent of it were false or genuine. It required no revulsion to elicit the admission that Christ's pardon was surer than his own; and might he not moreover be the unworthy instrument of such an act of grace? Was it really inconsistent of him to say:

> Myn hooly pardoun may yow alle warice. . . .
> I yow assoille, by myn heigh power. . . .
> And Jhesu Crist, that is oure soules leche,
> So graunte yow his pardoun to receyve,
> For that is best; I wol yow nat deceyve.
>
> (VI. 906–18)

Or, supposing he wished people to believe the first two statements while disbelieving or discounting them himself, why should he hesitate to add the prayer and the final assurance?

Under the supposition that Chaucer had originally ended here, having composed neither prologue nor epilogue, what would have been the effect of the tale over-all? Simply, that of a straight "moral tale"; with homiletic digressions against gluttony, gambling, and swearing; devoid of ironic cross-lighting, and marvellously impressive.

But, if the charge of humbug contained in the General Prologue were to be borne out, Chaucer could see that something further must be done. Let us suppose that he thereupon added the present conclusion. This, to be sure, is vividly effective; but it does not fundamentally alter the picture. It adds touches of humour to the character; it lets us know what Bailey thought of him; but it leaves the rest as before. What alternatives, then, were open to the poet if he wished to reveal unmistakably a deeper perfidy in the Pardoner? Obviously, the hypocrite would have to be exposed either by others or by himself. If by others, there would have to be a good deal of dramatic action, within a narrative frame— as later exemplified in the Canon's Yeoman's Tale; and this would be cumbrous and unwieldy. Or else the procedure would have to be by charge and countercharge, as in the Friar–Summoner quarrel, where it is a case of name–calling, with nothing much settled either way. But if the give–away was to be by the Pardoner himself, it would have to be brought about either, again, in dramatic action or by the device of confession. The first of these latter alternatives could hardly be managed economically, without considerable editorial interposition. But the device of confession was dramatic, immediate, and readily available. It was adumbrated in the religious practice of every believer, and anchored securely in old literary conventions that would maintain their

vitality down through Elizabethan tragedy and, with gradual trans-
formation, far beyond. Without it, Dante himself could have made no
headway; and Richard III and Macbeth would be inexplicable. For,
of course, soliloquy is but the pretence of a concession to realism—as
is likewise its modern extension, that written soliloquy set down as the
"stream of consciousness." The confessional device, in fact, leapt to
Chaucer's hand when he wished to reveal the naked inwardness of
character, as the Reeve, the Wife, the Merchant, and the Pardoner all
show; and neither he nor his contemporaries were aware of the fetters
that we retrospectively try to fasten upon them. Here, then, he was
uninhibited in resorting to a means of exposition so fully sanctioned;
and the Pardoner, in consequence, is equally uninhibited in his boastful self-denunciation:

> Thus spitte I out my venym under hewe
> Of hoolynesse, to semen hooly and trewe.
>
> (VI. 421–22)

Chaucer, we may continue to suppose, wrote the confession last, and
the Pardoner's infamy was now fully displayed.

But what, probably, had hardly been foreseen was the effect of this
on all that followed. For now the preaching seems a continual and
monstrous mockery, rising to blasphemy whenever the name of Christ
is uttered. This is an irony too profound for humanity, and we simply
recoil from belief in its possibility. We cannot credit the Pardoner's
total repudiation of the meaning to which he has given such sensitive
and moving expression. The combination is inconceivable. We are sure
his imagination and his morality are both enlisted on the side of good.
When he calls the rioters cursed men, when he says of one of them,

> And atte laste the feend, oure enemy,
> Putte in his thought that he sholde poyson beye,
> With which he myghte sleen his felawes tweye.
>
> (VI. 844–46),

we know he is not mocking. And when, therefore, he prays that his
present auditory may receive Christ's pardon, all of us believe that the
wish is sincere and devoid of irony.

But when the Pardoner goes on to advertise his wares to the same
company, we experience a rude shock. We seem to have been jolted
out of our moral assurance. We have heard all this before in a context
that made sense. Now it is as if a phonograph needle had been jarred
suddenly back into an earlier groove, and the sense is ruptured. How
can he possibly be saying to the people before whom he has just un-
covered his frauds:

> But, sires, o word forgat I in my tale:
> I have relikes and pardoun in my male. . . .
> If any of yow wole, of devocion,
> Offren, and han myn absolucion,
> Com forth anon, and kneleth heere adoun,
> And mekely receyveth my pardoun.
>
> (VI. 919–26)

So gross an affront to the meanest intelligence among the pilgrims is simply unimaginable. Certainly, it gives no comfort to those critics who think the Pardoner intelligent.

Why may not the answer to the puzzle lie in the conditions of composition? The tale, surely, was written first, and like almost every other finished piece in the whole work, it was originally rounded off with a pious sentiment:

> And lo, sires, thus I preche.
> And Jhesu Crist, that is oure soules leche,
> So graunte yow his pardoun to receyve,
> For that is best; I wol yow nat deceyve.
>
> (VI. 915–18)

It was entirely acceptable as the sort of performance the Pardoner might be expected to offer. Then Chaucer, we may suppose, wrote the headlink—not the prologue—and the conclusion, which framed the sermon in a vividly dramatic context, but without distorting the tale. Offering the relics and absolution was in character, as was the half-banter of the self-advertisement that accompanied the offer. There was no psychological break, for the Pardoner was yet strictly accurate in saying that he had hitherto omitted to speak of his relics and pardons. His references to them had been addressed to an imaginary audience of humble folk, good men and wives: "And lo, sires, thus I preche."

But then the poet, feeling perhaps that the tale came in awkwardly or too abruptly after the headlink with its indicated pause for refreshment, or sensing that the Pardoner's character was deserving of much fuller treatment; and wishing moreover to lengthen this block of narrative to the customary hour to hour-and-a-quarter's reading-time (for all Chaucer's writing is demonstrably conditioned by this simple and primary rule of oral delivery) wrote the Pardoner's confession, and at a stroke created a series of problems which have strained the best abilities of several generations of critics suckled on psychological realism. The ensuing game has been very exciting; but one surmises that the character that has been constructed of the "famous pulpit orator," so intellectual, so subtle, so racked with psychic turmoil, so pathetic, so sinister, would have astounded its original creator, and must be largely discounted as a modern instance. It is the poet's own fault, this time; but in any event, we have seen again (as in the Monk's Tale) how surprising and unexpected may be the results of altering one of the constituents of a cluster that combines conventional with naturalistic effects.

The Pardoner's Sermon and Its *Exemplum*

by Ralph W. V. Elliott

The scene of the Pardoner's *exemplum* is laid in a tavern, which leads him naturally enough into a harangue against three of the principal sins likely to be met in a tavern. There is, of course, the added piquancy of the fact that all this is taking place in the tavern on the road to Canterbury: the drinking pilgrims and the swearing Host must have been aware of the relevance of the Pardoner's eloquent diatribe, especially as they were several times directly addressed (573, 648, 660). It is characteristic of Chaucer's art in *The Canterbury Tales* thus fully to exploit an ironic situation created within the poem.

The tone of this moral disquisition is very different from that of the previous part of the Pardoner's address. Its heightened rhetoric, well illustrated by the frequent use of *o, lo, allas* and by the parade of biblical and other learning, offers a subtler key to the Pardoner's personal depravity than the simple, direct diction of the opening scene. Chaucer chose the latter mode as the means of complete and uninhibited self-exposure; he now chooses the former mode as the more appropriate instrument of hypocrisy. On the face of it, the condemnation of gluttony and gambling and swearing is all that it ought to be: eloquent:

> O wombe! O bely! O stynkyng cod,
> Fulfilled of dong and of corrupcioun!
> (534–35)

learned:

> Looke eek that to the kyng Demetrius,
> The kyng of Parthes, as the book seith us . . .
> (621–22)

"*The Pardoner's Sermon and Its* Exemplum" (*Editor's title*). *From* The Nun's Priest's Tale and the Pardoner's Tale (Geoffrey Chaucer), *by Ralph W. V. Elliott*, Notes on English Literature (*Oxford: Basil Blackwell, 1965*), *pp. 52–66. Copyright © 1965 by Basil Blackwell & Mott Ltd. Reprinted by permission of the publisher. Line numbers have been altered to those of Robinson's edition.*

convincing:

> For dronkenesse is verray sepulture
> Of mannes wit and his discrecioun.
>
> (558–59)

moving:

> The apostel wepyng seith ful pitously . . .
>
> (529)

sincere:

> Now, for the love of Crist, that for us dyde,
> Lete youre othes, bothe grete and smale.
>
> (658–59)

But following on the first scene of the performance which we have only just witnessed, the effect of this sudden switch from confession to pretence is overwhelming. In scene 2 the Pardoner is playing a completely different role and his virtuosity as an actor cannot but command our admiration. If we could only switch off our moral sense for a while it would indeed be "joye" to see his "bisynesse" (399). But we cannot switch it off, nor does Chaucer mean us to. The accomplished preacher so eloquently parading the vices of the tavern before our eyes is still the same who a few minutes earlier blandly declared that his

> entente is nat but for to wynne,
> And nothyng for correccioun of synne.
>
> (403–4)

"Nothyng for correccioun of synne"—then why this display of rhetoric and mock-virtue? Well, in part of course we are still being treated to a sample sermon; but partly the Pardoner, inspired by the ale-house environment in which he was performing, was no doubt working up towards the grand finale of his act, softening up the Host in particular for the final joke. Does he not single the Host out for special address (648) as the most apt recipient of the biblical warning paraphrased in 649–50, just as at the end of the first scene the mention of "a draughte of corny ale" (456) echoes the Host's earlier use of the same words in line 315 of the Link preceding *The Pardoner's Tale*? That in each of the first two scenes there is a line or two alluding to the Host is no accident; it shows the careful construction of Chaucer's poem as he works his way towards the climax.

But the disquisition on the vices of the tavern is not all pretence; here also the Pardoner is made to reveal himself directly in order to remind us that it is still the same actor we are watching. His display of learning shows that he is not one of "the lewed peple," and his

knowledge of good food and wine, used so eloquently to rail against
gluttony, is a logical consequence of the "coveityse" (424, 433) to which
he is so patently addicted:

> Nay, I wol drynke licour of the vyne.   (452)

Even the patronizing tone of the prologue creeps in:

> Nat Samuel, but Lamuel, seye I.   (585)

As a piece of pulpit oratory this portion of *The Pardoner's Tale*
shows Chaucer's art at its most versatile. We have already noted the
effectiveness of the exclamations which characterize the opening; but
it is not only through the repetition of *o, lo, allas,* that a sense of
urgency, almost of doom, is created. The key-words of this address are
similarly hammered home until they ring in our ears with frightening
intensity: *glotonye, hasard, hasardrye, othes, sweryng.* At times the
hammer blows are continuous, line by line:

> Gret *sweryng* is a thyng abhominable,
> And fals *sweryng* is yet moore reprevable.
> The heighe God forbad *sweryng* at al,
> Witnesse on Mathew; but in special
> Of *sweryng* seith the hooly Jeremye,
> "Thou shalt *swere* sooth thyne othes, and nat lye,
> And *swere* in doom, and eek in rightwisnesse";
> But ydel *sweryng* is a cursednesse.   (631–38)

This sense of urgency is underlined by the repeated invitation to
"looke" and "bihoold" (578, 579, 621, 639), invitations surely meant
to be accompanied by the Pardoner's "busy" use of gestures as he
speaks:

> Thanne peyne I me to strecche forth the nekke,
> And est and west upon the peple I bekke,
>   (395–96)

and given emphasis by being placed at the beginning of lines or para-
graphs. Similar emphasis is created by starting a paragraph with a
proper name (488, 492, 505, 603), ringing it out as a shot is fired from
a pistol, emphatically, commandingly, as if to silence all opposition.
Appealing to the Bible, to learned authors or to history, was a favourite
medieval method of argument. Chauntecleer the cock makes full use
of it in *The Nun's Priest's Tale,* and there, too, Chaucer uses the exclamatory *lo* and *looke* as pointers to the names being invoked.

The high eloquence of the Pardoner's harangue is balanced by
several colloquial turns of phrase which are characteristic of Chaucer's
style; expressions which add continuity and a feeling of orderly prog-

ress to the sense, but which are sufficiently inconspicuous not to deflate
the oratory or jar the listener or reader into a feeling of incongruity.
Such are the phrases which end one argument and begin another and
which we soon learn to recognize as typical Chaucerisms:

> Namoore of this, for it may wel suffise.   (588)
> Now wol I speke of othes . . .   (629)
> . . . now wol I telle forth my tale.   (660)

The last nine lines of this scene (895–903) serve as an epilogue, a
conclusion and summing-up, to both parts of this central section of
The Pardoner's Tale, the moral disquisition and the tale of the three
revellers. After the fluent narrative style of the tale we are back in the
exclamatory rhetoric of the earlier outburst against the sins of the
tavern. Six times *o* and *allas* recur in these nine lines in a deliberate
echoing of their previous occurrences, and the key-words are there also:

> O *glotonye,* luxurie, and *hasardrye!* . . .
> And *othes* grete.   (897, 899)

The scene ends with a final hypocritical flourish in the form of a
rhetorical question, and with splendid appropriateness on the word
allas which envelops, as it were, the last four lines:

> *Allas!* mankynde, how may it bitide
> That to thy creatour, which that the wroghte,
> And with his precious herte-blood thee boghte,
> Thou art so fals and so unkynde, *allas?*
>
> (900–903)

The effectiveness of the twofold *allas* is enhanced by the rhyming
mankynde and *unkynde* no less deliberately positioned, and the many
vowel sounds which would be pronounced long in Chaucer's English
add further to the almost chant-like effect of these lines.

In the final scene of *The Pardoner's Tale* the sermon is concluded
in the appropriate medieval manner and the joke against the Host is
played out.

The sermon ends with the application of text and *exemplum* to the
conduct of the congregation and with a concluding prayer-formula.
With the mention of "goode men" (904) and "ye wyves" (910) we are
back with the Pardoner's imaginary village audience. Once more the
talk is of buying and selling pardons, of offering money and wool

> or elles silver broches, spoones, rynges,   (908)

in exchange for salvation. Once more the slick salesman pits his superior wits against the credulous, superstitious faith of "the lewed
peple."

It is a brief, businesslike conclusion, a sharp contrast to the lofty lines which ended the preceding tale. With a final ironic touch the Pardoner warns his imaginary audience against the sin of avarice in the same breath that invites them to satisfy his greed. The key-word now is *offre* (907, 910, 914). Absolution is available for those "that wol offre," potentially therefore for everyone present (cp. 430–31) except the preacher himself. For him there is only the one gospel:

> Thus kan I preche agayn that same vice
> Which that I use, and that is avarice.
>
> (427–28)

He said so, proudly, in his prologue, and with the same self-satisfied flourish he now concludes his commentary to the pilgrims:

> And lo, sires, thus I preche.   (915)

The concluding formula (916–18) has been regarded by some critics as inconsistent with both the preceding offer of pardons for sale to the villagers and the following offer to the pilgrims, particularly the Host. But there is really nothing inconsistent in it. Admittedly, these lines have the ring of sincerity in them, but so do the many conventional medieval formulas to which this conforms and which were often uttered without much thought for their content or relevance. *The Nun's Priest's Tale,* for example, ends on a very similar note:

> Now, goode God, if that it be thy wille,
> As seith my lord, so make us alle goode men,
> And brynge us to his heighe blisse! Amen.
>
> (VII. 3444–46)

Moreover, it is important to remember that the Pardoner has only just finished advertising his own pardons as a key to salvation: anyone who "offered," that is paid, was assured of "the blisse of hevene" (912), in other words, of Christ's pardon. Thus whoever wanted the "best" of which the concluding formula speaks (918) could buy it from him.

But even the ring of sincerity may be spurious. Did the Pardoner himself, lost soul that he was, believe what he was saying? The irony of "Cristes hooly werk" (340) for example, or the hypocritical allusions to Christ's sacrifice in 501, 658 and 902, will surely have put us on our guard against suddenly taking the Pardoner's reference to Christ at its face value, particularly in the context of a conventional formula. To suggest, as some critics have done, that the Pardoner suddenly sees the error of his ways, recognizes the inadequacy of his pardons, and becomes at the eleventh hour a reformed character, is to misunderstand him completely. Whatever may be the significance of the reference to Christ's pardon (and in a conventional concluding formula there may

not have been any at all), the Pardoner's "I wol yow nat deceyve" (918)
is just about the last thing we are prepared to believe of this scoundrel.
After his repeated assertions to the contrary, after the "hundred false
japes" (394), after his shameless self-exposure, his hypocritical rhetoric
and his slick sales talk, we know one thing for certain about him,
namely that he lives for deceit "and nothyng for correccioun of synne"
(404). His final comment becomes the crowning irony of his whole
performance.

As for what follows, the offer of pardons to the Canterbury pilgrims
and the invitation to the Host to come forward to "kisse the relikes
everychon" (944), it is a joke. I have already suggested . . . that the
earlier allusions to the Host are part of Chaucer's preparation for this
concluding episode, and that the whole tone of the passage is jocular.
. . . After all that has gone before the comic finale is both a relief
leading appropriately to laughter (961) and a fitting retribution for
the Pardoner: despite all his eloquence and "gift of the gab" he is
left speechless (956–57). The performance is over, the Host "wol no
lenger pleye" (958), and it is just as well that it is all finished. In the
Knight's words:

> Namoore of this, for it is right ynough!   (962)

The Tale

The Pardoner's tale proper, that is the story of the three revellers
and the old man searching for death, extends from line 661 to line 894.
The rest of what we have called scene 2 of the Pardoner's performance
[135–575] is given over, you will remember, to the disquisition on
gluttony, gambling, and swearing, except for lines 463–84 and 895–903.
These passages both serve a dual purpose as prologue and epilogue re-
spectively to tale and disquisition alike.

The opening lines (463–84) set the scene of the tale in Flanders and
paint a background of sinful abandon at the same time as leading
naturally enough into the eloquent denunciation of the sins of the
tavern which is set off by the exclamatory *lo* at the beginning of line
485.

The concluding lines (895–903) which serve as epilogue to tale and
disquisition, we have already discussed. . . .

When the Pardoner returns to his tale at line 661, the background
is taken for granted, and we are precipitated into the action in the
first sentence. This element of urgency is a feature of the whole tale.
There is no need to be puzzled by line 661, as some readers have been,
because there has been no previous reference to the three "riotoures."
Chaucer must often have worked at great speed, as both the sheer
quantity of his work as well as occasional signs of haste suggest. He

had introduced "yonge folk" who frequented taverns in 463 ff. and may well have forgotten what details he had given and not troubled to look back when he resumed the tale at line 661. But any difficulty disappears if we understand the line to mean "these revellers, three of whom I am talking about," which is a legitimate rendering. The story makes it clear that there were other people present at the tavern.

The story of two or three villains who kill each other after finding a treasure was an old one already in Chaucer's time. Some versions were current in far eastern countries more than two thousand years ago, and during the Middle Ages the story was current in many European countries. Chaucer often took such familiar stories and refashioned them for his own purposes, as he did, for example, with the old fable of the cock and the fox in *The Nun's Priest's Tale*. In the case of *The Pardoner's Tale* the explicit association with avarice is found in other versions, and the old man who figures in Chaucer's story may have been suggested to him by the figure of a hermit who in some versions finds the treasure which is then appropriated by the avaricious villains. But Chaucer's version is no mere copy or simple re-telling of the familiar story. He not only fits the story admirably into the framework of the Pardoner's performance, and adds weight to it by the disquisition on the sins of the tavern, but he also alters the whole direction of the story by introducing the motive of the search for death.

In other versions the story is a straightforward *exemplum* of the biblical text that "the love of money is the root of all evil," the same text which the Pardoner invariably uses (333–34, 425–26). Chaucer's tale has the same moral, as it functions as an *exemplum* in the Pardoner's sermon, but its significance extends further: the contrast between the three young villains rushing headlong to perdition and the old man seeking peace for his weary bones serves as a profound comment on human life. The young men are full of vigour and energy, but they are blind. They cannot see that their fate is in their own hands; they cannot see where their evil dispositions, their selfishness, their greed, their dishonesty towards one another, are leading them. By contrast, the old man is feeble and helpless, but he can see the truth. He can see that his fate is in God's hands (726); he can distinguish between good and evil, between right and wrong. He, too, is looking for death, but he will not accept death through sin in the form in which it is to be found at the foot of the oak-tree. He must rather continue his wandering until it will please mother earth to respond to his pathetic cry "leet me in!" (731).

The mysteriously "forwrapped" figure (718) of the old man has fascinated all readers of *The Pardoner's Tale* and puzzled many. Who is he? Whom does he represent? He cannot be meant as an impersonation of death, as some critics have suggested, because he is himself seeking death. His strangely restless seeking suggests perhaps a figure like that of the legendary Wandering Jew condemned to walk the earth until the Day of Judgment in a fruitless search for death. But there is no real need to attempt to identify the old man; his effective presence in the poem is its own justification. He represents not only a true vision of death, but his very appearance suggests the closeness of death which the revellers are too blind to see. Such advanced old age as is here so graphically portrayed means that death is just around the corner and is of course intended as a warning to the three young villains to mend their ways while yet there is time. They are too blinded, however, to heed the warning. They see only a doddering old man, and so they rush madly along the "croked wey" (761) towards the death they were *not* seeking:

> And everich of thise riotoures ran
> Til he cam to that tree.
>
> (768–69)

The tale is full of such irony. The villains seek death but do not recognize him when they find him; and when unwittingly they stumble across him, in the shape of "floryns fyne of gold ycoyned rounde" (770), then they stop seeking him:

> No lenger thanne after Deeth they soughte.   (772)

There is irony also in the swearing of oaths of which the tale is full. Swearing is one of the sins of the tavern against which the Pardoner is preaching and the three villains are experts at it:

> And many a grisly ooth thanne han they sworn,
> And Cristes blessed body al torente,—
>
> (708–9)

a clear echo, you will notice, of lines 472–75. The climax of all this swearing is the oath of brotherhood which the three men swear as they set out on their quest,

> to lyve and dyen ech of hem for oother.   (703)

Before the night is over it is not Death that is slain, as they solemnly swear in 699–701, but each of them has died at his sworn brother's hand!

The pace of the narrative goes hand in hand with the rapidity of the action. Within the first five lines (661–65) we are thoroughly involved. A handful of words (*riotoures, taverne, cors, grave*) conjure forth the appropriate atmosphere and precipitate the story into action. The movement carries us steadily forward to the meeting with the old man, the finding of the gold, the mutual betrayal, the slaying. There are no digressions, none of the displays of learned authors so

dear to the medieval storyteller, none of the discursive discussions of
favourite topics so dear to Chaucer. Everything is strictly organized,
economical, relevant, a superb short story in verse. Its length is about
the same as that of the Pardoner's immediately preceding moral disquisition, but in style, in movement and diction, the two passages are
strikingly different. In place of the eloquent rhetoric, the learned allusions and forceful repetitions, the tale relies for effect upon an easily
flowing verse and a simple narrative vocabulary. There are repetitions,
as we might expect, for this is a favourite device of Chaucer's: much is
made, for instance, of the word *slay* (673, 676, 679, 686, 699, 700); and
there are the familiar meaningful echoes of words, as when the "faire"
florins and "this precious hoord" (774–75) are echoed a few lines later
by "Goddes precious dignitee" and "so fair a grace" (782–83), an echo
all the more poignant for the irony which it lays bare.

The contrast between the three villains and the old man is sharpened
by a choice of telling words. The latter is old and poor and meek
(713–14) and his mode of address is courteous. The former are dif-
ferentiated from each other only as "the proudeste" (716), "the worste"
(776), and "the yongeste" (804); to the old man they are overbearing,
crudely impolite, answering his gentle "lordes" and "sires" (715, 739,
760) with a rude "carl" (717) and "olde cherl" (750) despite his mild
remonstrance.

Much of the tale is dialogue, but it is narrative dialogue, that is, it
advances the action as much as the straight narrative does. Only the
old man's first speech stands out in sharp relief against the steady pace
of the remainder; appropriately enough, for he is old and moves slowly
and his words reflect his senile pace as he pathetically taps his staff
against the ground.

The Pardoner's is a moving tale, and for a moment near its beginning we even find ourselves in sympathy with the three young men
who are anxious to rid the world of one who

> hath a thousand slayn this pestilence.   (679)

But the sympathy, if it exists at all, is shortlived. After the boy's and
the taverner's macabre accounts of the pestilence with their reiteration
of *slayn* comes the revellers' first outburst. Now the vile oaths take
over, drowning even the threefold *sleen-slayn-sleeth* in 699–700:
"Goddes armes!" (692), "Goddes digne bones!" (695), "Goddes dignitee" (701). The language becomes vulgar and provocative, although
the deathly undercurrent persists. We hardly need Chaucer's reference
to their drunken rage and their blasphemous swearing (705, 708–9) to
turn from the villains in disgust. Our revulsion is complete as we
read the encounter between them and the meek old man whose pitiful
state now commands our sympathy. By introducing the old man into
the story at this point Chaucer was not merely following older versions

of the tale; he was using him to establish the two poles of good and evil in the world of this tale at the very moment when the villains are unwittingly within sight of the goal which earlier on we might have thought a worthy one. After the finding of the gold we witness the betrayal with a morbid fascination which is a tribute to Chaucer's narrative skill. When the end comes Chaucer's economy is masterly: he dismisses the death agonies of the two poisoned wretches with a cool reference to appropriate literature on poisoning and "thus ended" the two of them. Had we been treated to some of these harrowing details we might have felt another pang of sympathy for the villains. So Chaucer took no risks. And we are left with a strong sense that justice has been done.

And at this point, without break or warning, the Pardoner returns to the foreground with his lofty eloquence as his barrage of *o*'s launches him into the epilogue. The *exemplum* is finished, the sermon nearly done, the whole performance almost at an end.

Narrative Speed in the *Pardoner's Tale*

by David V. Harrington

A common gambit used, I will wager, by every teacher of Chaucer's *Pardoner's Tale* at one time or another, is to pose the question: Why does the Pardoner in his prologue speak out so candidly about his own cheating and hypocritical avarice? And all of us coax from our students what seem to us rational answers: the Pardoner wanted to boast; he was among sophisticated people very different from his usual victims; like most people on trips, he felt more garrulous than usual; he was drunk. Similarly, all of us test these solutions in the light of the astonishingly unexpected behavior by the Pardoner at the end of his tale as, having confessed, indeed bragged of, his deceit, he tries to sell his false relics to the pilgrims. We must resort to more complicated and sophisticated interpretations to justify this seemingly inconsistent behavior on the part of the Pardoner. Between these two passages, we encounter still other popular cruxes. But if we are diligent in plodding through our critical bibliographies, we can find a variety of interpretations defending the psychological integrity of Chaucer's creation. In fact, such commentary has been subtle and substantial enough to warrant two derisive essays by notable scholars within the past thirty years. Professors G. G. Sedgewick and Paull F. Baum ridicule at length, perhaps justly, the ingenious, psychological speculation by a host of distinguished scholars concerning hidden motives, complicated ironical relationships between the Pardoner and the rioters in his tale, or repressed feelings of sexual inadequacy in either the Pardoner or the Host; in short they deplore the tendency to offer anything but admissions that Chaucer could have been unaware of, or indifferent to, inconsistencies in the behavior of his character.[1] React-

---

"Narrative Speed in the Pardoner's Tale" by David V. Harrington. From Chaucer Review, III (1968–69), 50–59. Copyright © 1968 by The Pennsylvania State University. Reprinted by permission of The Pennsylvania State University Press.

[1] Both G. G. Sedgewick in "The Progress of Chaucer's Pardoner, 1880–1940," *MLQ* 1 (1940), 431–58; and Paull F. Baum in *Chaucer: A Critical Appreciation* (Durham, 1958), pp. 44–59, give helpful bibliographies of criticism of the *Pardoner's Tale*. Two key documents contributing to psychological analysis are G. L. Kittredge's *Chaucer and His Poetry* (Cambridge, Mass., 1915), pp. 155, 211–18; and R. M. Lumiansky, *Of Sondry Folk* (Austin, 1955), pp. 201–23.

ing, at least in part, to the same excess, Kemp Malone has suggested
that Chaucer sacrifices verisimilitude in the *Pardoner's Tale* for the
sake of following "the conventions of literature, the conventions of
his own day," one such convention being the narrator's self-revelation.
He goes on to postulate, however, that the Pardoner's is the only tale
in the *Canterbury Tales* that serves primarily to characterize its teller.
We are to see, "as nothing else could make us see, what manner of
man he is and how he preaches for to win." [2] I shall argue that the
value of the tale, as emphasized by its rhetoric, ultimately rises above
an appreciation of the narrator's character, whether realistic or not.

This value is basically the inexpressible emotion created in part by
the self-revealed character of the Pardoner, in part by his moralizing
and his tale, and ultimately by the striking contrast throughout between the recommended ideals and the actual behavior. This total
emotional effect comes across most powerfully during the moments of
reading or listening. Our discovery of the techniques of psychological
analysis, with the tendency to make cross references between different
parts of the poem and to scrutinize a character's motives for consistency,
detracts from the force of such emotional expression.

Chaucer's interest in psychological consistency is apparently rather
limited; the more impressive aesthetic values in the tale are not de-
pendent upon such consistency; in fact one can point to an abundance
of evidence within the tale suggesting the conscious employment of
artistic techniques aimed to produce effects very different from those
associated with psychological realism. All of this, in spite of the common agreement among scholars that the *Pardoner's Tale* is one of the
thoroughly defensible examples of what Lumiansky calls the "dramatic
principle" [3] in action.

We must make a concession, however. If the *Pardoner's Tale* is not
dramatic, neither are Shakespeare's plays. But, in speaking of dramatic
effects, let us reject A. C. Bradley's general approach to characterization
and take Harley Granville-Barker's instead.[4]

What I wish to suggest is that one needs to read Chaucer's more
dramatic Canterbury tales, including the Wife of Bath's, perhaps the
Merchant's, and certainly the Pardoner's, somewhat in the spirit of
Granville-Barker's instructions for study of a Shakespearean play. One
should recognize the fact that dramatic situations and character behavior are employed for their immediate momentary impression. To
cite a comparable problem in scholarship, while entranced by the
unfolding intrigue by which Iago leads Othello from doubt to cer-

[2] Kemp Malone, *Chapters on Chaucer* (Baltimore, 1951), pp. 211, 213.

[3] Lumiansky, *Of Sondry Folk*, pp. 5, 201–23.

[4] See A. C. Bradley's analysis of Othello's character in *Shakespearean Tragedy*
(Oxford, 1904), pp. 152–62; Harley Granville-Barker's discussion of "double time"
is in *Prefaces to Shakespeare*, II (Princeton, 1947), 24–30; see also pp. 112–14.

tainty of Desdemona's unfaithfulness, we are not really invited to trace the inconsistent references to time; if we add them up, we should not concern ourselves with the fact that Cassio and Desdemona could have had no time together alone since her very recent marriage to Othello. What is dramatically important in *Othello* is that the protagonist believes the deceiver and that we enjoy the dual effects of first, fearing for Othello in his delusion, and second, appreciating Iago's diabolical ingenuity. Similarly, much more important than the reasons for the Pardoner's confessions are the confessions themselves as an expression of complex but general human feeling.[5] In other words, recognition of the greatest values in the tale results from a rapid reading, by which I mean a reading with the impression or illusion of speeches and events following hard upon each other, not necessarily with more rapid pronunciation of words.

The difference is in the effect of being startled into a greater awareness by each successive scene, rather than one of pondering the meaning of all that which has thus far occurred. One should appreciate, not the Pardoner's subtlety, but his audacity. Slow, careful analysis, unless based squarely upon the experience of uninterrupted, sequential re-reading, detracts from this. One can sense much the same kind of loss in Sir Laurence Olivier's film version of *Richard III*. The scene of his wooing Anne in the movie is made more "realistic" when separated in time from the death of her father-in-law, Henry VI; but we lose much of the protagonist's monstrous effrontery, which is more apparent in a reading of the text of Shakespeare's play. It is in connection with a similar effect in the *Pardoner's Tale* that I turn away from Kittredge, Lumiansky, and other exponents of psychological character-analysis. The rhetoric or style contributes to sufficiently complicated and entrancing emotional effects so that the attentive reader has more than enough to concern himself with in admiring the narrator's combination of wit and crassness in speaking of his deceptiveness. The prevalence of rhetorical techniques contributing to the illusion of speed suggests that the Pardoner's occasionally odd behavior is more for the sake of immediate dramatic and aesthetic expressiveness than for psychological realism.

This is not to deny any conscious employment of psychology in the tale. The Pardoner knows, for example, how to appeal to avarice while preaching against the same thing; we see this when he discloses the manner in which he sells the shoulder-bone of the holy Jew's sheep, and the magic mitten, both sales promising material gains for farmers and the Pardoner (VI.350–76). He can sell such relics by making people appear to be sinners unless they rush up to buy (377–84). He can make

---

[5] My argument in its broad outline is obviously indebted to the aesthetic theories of Susanne K. Langer, especially as developed in *Feeling and Form* (New York, 1953).

life embarrassing for those who oppose him in any way by hinting at individuals in the congregation when denouncing sins (412–22). And he is fully aware of the contradiction in his own character, being wholly addicted to the one craving he preaches against (427–34). But all of these are immediately apparent psychological effects. There are no ponderable subtleties. One can catch the irony in each case without slackening the pace of his reading.

The generally unappreciated digression on tavern sins functions as a device to foreshadow later more dramatic expression of the same values. The force of this passage also can be felt through rapid reading rather than through consideration of possible analogies in moral treatises of the same vintage. One might hesitate to say that this preliminary material, with the exhortations against gluttony, gambling, and swearing (463–660), means literally, *"Radix malorum est Cupiditas."* But the rioters at the start are drinking in the tavern, and, after they find the gold, they desire wine to while away the time until sundown; hence gluttony. They indicate at one point that they especially want the gold so that they might "pleye at dees right at oure owene wille"; hence gambling. And they swear oaths, later broken, to be brothers just before they go out to slay Death; hence swearing. This is an admittedly facile solution for this part of the tale. But let us go on.

Even the much debated question of the relationship of the tale to the sermon tradition of Chaucer's time loses much of its urgency.[6] Aesthetically, the exact relationship of the tale proper to the pattern of medieval sermons is of little importance. We need to imagine, of course, the tale being told with the dual intent of both warning against avarice and helping the Pardoner satisfy his own avarice by the favorable effect it has. We need at least the illusion of a rather complicated sermon atmosphere. The narrator, however, gives us plenty of preparation for this:

> But though myself be gilty in that synne,
> Yet kan I maken oother folk to twynne
> From avarice, and soore to repente.
> But that is nat my principal entente. . . .
>
> (429–32)

Our admiration for the moral excellence of the tale as it unfolds combines with our contempt for the hypocrisy of the teller to give an impression of dynamic form with a tension between opposing emotional appeals, the type of tension often identified as a vital quality for all

---

[6] See Nancy H. Owen, "The Pardoner's Introduction, Prologue, and Tale; Sermon and *Fabliau*," *JEGP*, LXVI (1967), 541–49, for a convenient recent summary of this debate.

great art. This tension, which is also a form of ironic ambiguity, is apparent to all readers; but our acceptance of it results particularly from the rapidity and cogency of the Pardoner's narrative style. We could only deride his futility and hypocrisy if his tale were ineffectual. Instead, the rapid movement and earnestness of the message impress us, in spite of our awareness of the narrator's "ful vicious" character. This point necessitates a more detailed discussion of rhetoric.

The nature of the tale and the personal character of the Pardoner make inadvisable the use of dilatory transitional devices, such as those in more leisurely narratives, such as the *Knight's Tale,* the *Man of Law's Tale,* or *Troilus and Criseyde.* The narrator wishes to convince us by the forcefulness of his sermon, not by impressing upon us the profundity of his argument. He gives the impression of knowing only one tale; but he knows it well, as he says "For I kan al by rote that I telle" (332). The result is a rapid movement, a complete lack of hesitation, as the narrator moves from one scene to another; no dependency upon authority is apparent (except of course in his liberal references to historical and Biblical figures as illustrations for his themes). One can easily visualize the skinny Pardoner swiftly reciting his memorized narrative.

In the *Knight's Tale,* for example, it is easy to find transitions like the following:

> Now wol I stynte of Palamon a lite,
> And lete hym in his prisoun stille dwelle,
> And of Arcita forth I wol yow telle.

or:

> And in this blisse lete I now Arcite,
> And speke I wole of Palamon a lite.
>   (I.1334–36, 1449–50)

In the *Man of Law's Tale,* we also find frequent deliberate attempts to give an impression of narrative coherence, as in the following example:

> Now wolde som men waiten, as I gesse,
> That I sholde tellen al the purveiance
> That th'Emperour, of his grete noblesse,
> Hath shapen for his doghter, dame Custance.
>   (II.246–49)

All such transitions slow the movement, inviting us to ponder the relationships between different parts of the narrative. But formal transitions are hard to find in either the Pardoner's prologue or the tale. Sometimes only a word or short phrase can be discerned, as "Heere is a miteyn *eek,* that ye may se" (372). In another rare instance,

the narrator refers to his refusal to absolve women who have made
their husbands cuckolds, with the short phrase *"By this gaude* have I
wonne, yeer by yeer . . ."* (389). Only one example of a formal, deliberate transition occurs in the prologue: "But shortly myn entente
I wol devyse . . ." (423). Even in the long series of digressions shortly
after he begins his tale, there is remarkably little use of transitional
devices as he moves from one illustration or apostrophe to another.
Occasionally they do appear:

> But herkneth, lordynges, o word, I yow preye. . . .   (573)

> Namoore of this, for it may wel suffise.
> And now that I have spoken of glotonye,
> Now wol I yow deffenden hasardrye.
>   (588–90)

> Now wol I speke of othes false and grete. . . .   (629)

In general, however, in view of the numerous shifts of emphasis as he
swings from the introductory scene to the digressions on gluttony,
gambling, and swearing and back to the tale again, we can say that
the narrator seldom employs transitions. In fact, we find frequent use
of *asyndeton,* the omission of transitions,[7] to give the effect of breath-
less haste and roughness. He packs main clauses together in series; he
moves abruptly from phase to phase of his argument. In an illustrative
passage on drunkenness, he apostrophizes the drunkard, cataloguing
disgusting details with brief clauses joined in a series, and then ironically and abruptly, with no transition, reproves the generic drunkard
for his lack of discretion:

> O dronke man, disfigured is thy face,
> Sour is thy breeth, foul artow to embrace,
> And thurgh thy dronke nose semeth the soun
> As though thou seydest ay "Sampsoun, Sampsoun!"
> And yet, God woot, Sampsoun drank nevere no wyn.
> Thou fallest as it were a styked swyn;
> Thy tonge is lost, and al thyn honeste cure;
> For dronkenesse is verray sepulture
> Of mannes wit and his discrecioun.
>   (551–59)

Furthermore, in his moral digression, the narrator joins short im-
peratives within expository themes with no formal connectives:

> Gret sweryng is a thyng abhominable,
> And fals sweryng is yet moore reprevable.

---

[7] See J. W. H. Atkin's summary of Geoffrey de Vinsauf's medieval poetic in *English
Literary Criticism: The Medieval Phase* (Gloucester, Mass., 1952), pp. 200–3.

> The heighe God forbad sweryng at al,
> *Witnesse on Mathew.* . . .
>
> (631–34)

Somewhat related to Chaucer's use of *asyndeton* in this tale is his employment of *hyperbaton,* an unnatural order of words and ideas. The effect of *hyperbaton* may be to aid in emphasizing the narrator's excited or disordered state of mind, or, more specifically, in the case of the Pardoner, to reveal his drunkenness. But another effect, and a more important one so far as the purpose of this study is concerned, is to contribute to the hurried crowding of ideas and images in a rapidly progressing discourse. The narrator never actually loses control of his material within the tale itself. But in a few places he introduces material in inversions, in awkwardly positioned nominative absolutes, or in unconnected groups or series used much as nominative absolutes. Occasionally, interrupting elements obscure the structure of his sentences.

In the description of the effort of cooks to satisfy gluttonous desire, an inverted series of modifying prepositional phrases creates a dual effect of haste and emphasis: "Of spicerie of leef, and bark, and roote/ Shal been his sauce ymaked by delit . . ." (544–45). Occasionally the narrator begins a sentence with a substantive, presumably the subject of a clause separated from its verb by an interruption, which is replaced by a pronoun as the subject, thus leaving the substantive as an absolute:

> *Herodes,* whoso wel the stories soghte,
> Whan he of wyn was repleet at his feeste,
> Right at his owene table *he* yaf his heeste
> To sleen the Baptist John, ful giltelees.
>
> (488–91)

And also "This wise *philosophre,* thus seyde *hee* (620). The narrator exemplifies his discourse on swearing with several choice examples in a series not grammatically connected to his sentence:

> "By Goddes precious herte," and "By his nayles,"
> And "By the blood of Crist that is in Hayles,
> Sevene is my chaunce, and thyn is cynk and treye!"
> "By Goddes armes, if thou falsly pleye,
> This daggere shal thurghout thyn herte go!"—
> This fruyt cometh of the bicched bones two,
> Forsweryng, ire, falsnesse, homycide.
>
> (651–57)

The absence of conjunctions (*asyndeton*) and the variations from normal sentence order (*hyperbaton*) occur for the most part in the

digression rather than in the story of the revellers and the gold. Most
of the narrative portion is in dialogue; actions follow one another in
a rapid sequence, and little rhetorical ornamentation is employed or
necessary. A. C. Spearing offers assistance on this point: "The pace of
the narrative, . . . gradually increasing to an almost grotesque violence, . . . is expressive of the very nature of the story." [8] Within the
narrative there are frequently words and phrases denoting hurried
movement: " 'Go bet,' quod he, 'and axe redily . . .'" (667); "And up
they stirte, al dronken in this rage" (705); "And everich of thise
riotoures ran . . ." (768). And the spareness of the context within
which such actions occur augments this effect of rapid, unhampered
movement.

A minimum of description of either persons or places appears in the
tale proper told by the Pardoner. The characters are anonymous and
largely symbolic. In fact, the narrator avoids an almost unavoidable
opportunity to name a character in the scene where one of rioters tells
the boy to ask "What cors is this that passeth heer forby" (668). The
boy only describes him as "an old felawe of youres" (672). The three
rioters are called by such names as "the worste of hem," "the yongeste
of hem alle," and "that oother." Even the much discussed old man,
who directs the three men to the pile of gold, is given no name and is
described, in very general terms, as an old man with a "pale and
welked" face. He appears suddenly as a startling contrast in personal
values to the rioters, functions also to direct them to the scene of their
next action in the drama, and disappears from the stage as mysteriously
as Lear's Fool, with no further duties required of him.

The scene is vaguely set in Flanders in a town which has at least a
tavern and an apothecary shop, but with no description of the town
or countryside. Obviously action and dialogue are paramount in the
progress of this tale. The "compaignye of yonge folk" are described
only by their activities. They haunted such folly "As riot, hasard,
stywes, and tavernes," etc. (465–82). The sinful actions of Lot, Herod,
Adam, the drunkard who says "Sampsoun, Sampsoun!", Attila, and
King Demetrius of Parthia are plainly narrated without description
in the moral digression. The story itself is largely limited to dialogue
with very brief generalized expository statements. All of these observa-
tions are in marked contrast with such poems as the *Knight's Tale* and
the *Man of Law's Tale*; but of course they contrast differently in each
case. The *Knight's Tale,* with its preponderance of physical and active
description, and the *Man of Law's Tale,* with its emphasis upon moral
and spiritual evaluations, differ sharply from the blunt, matter-of-fact
statements in the *Pardoner's Tale.* Even other tales usually thought of

[8] A. C. Spearing, ed., *The Pardoner's Prologue and Tale* (Cambridge, 1965), pp.
35–37.

as moving swiftly and directly to their conclusions, like the Miller's and Reeve's or even the Physician's, are structured with a very orderly sequence of events, rather than making special use of rhetorical devices for the impression of speed. The descriptions of the carpenter's wife, of Symkyn and his wife, of Virginia, are not really hurried. The rhetoric of the *Pardoner's Tale* sets it apart from the others. Agreeing with scholarly tradition, we can say that the character of the Pardoner, in coordination with this rhetoric, also unquestionably contributes dash and flavor to the tale as a whole, but because of a remarkable heightening of dominant traits, not because of realistic characterization.

To follow through with this approach, the reader should interpret each shift in the Pardoner's behavior as part of a pattern dramatizing the conjunction of superb moralizing with depraved personality. If we permit the rhetorical devices aimed at speed to have their effect, the old problems of reconciling the Pardoner's motives at each stage of his narrative with all that has gone before tend to disappear. With this approach even the conclusion can be understood. Immediately following the tale of three rioters, the narrator inserts an emotional apostrophe denouncing the whole range of sins: "O cursed synne of alle cursednesse!" etc. (895–903), following which he promptly enters into his spiel, presumably aimed at his usual rural audiences:

> Boweth youre heed under this hooly bulle!
> Cometh up, ye wyves, offreth of youre wolle!
>
> (909–10)

This, however, is followed by the confidential admission of a very genuine pardon, over which he has no control:

> . . . And lo, sires, thus I preche.
> And Jhesu Crist, that is oure soules leche,
> So graunte yow his pardoun to receyve,
> For that is best; I wol yow nat deceyve.
>
> (915–18)

In a famous comment, Kittredge referred to this part of the Pardoner's speech as "a very paroxysm of agonized sincerity," which can last only a moment,[9] just before the Pardoner's jesting and quarreling with the Host. My contention is that this alternating between sincerity and crass salesmanship is for the sake of keeping before us the ironic contrast. We are to be reminded at every step of the juxtaposition of contradictory values. These contrasts tend not so much to clarify the Pardoner as to set before us in as powerful and abstract terms as possible the quality of feeling associated with our recognition of contradictions in practice and ideals. Chaucer, in anticipation of Shake-

---

[9] Kittredge, *The Poetry of Chaucer*, p. 217.

speare, and like most great poets, should be given credit for intentionally distorting characterization for the sake of emphasizing this particular aspect of humanity.

It is not necessary then to think of the Pardoner as a real person. He is merely a creation of the poet, a contrivance, for the sake of helping communicate the rather complicated emotion expressed by the ironic structure of the combined prologue and tale. The unity of the piece is in this emotion as it reveals itself during the progress of the narrative, not in consistency of characterization. The personality of the Pardoner, without question, fascinates us; but such fascination results from his keeping in balance before us such theoretically irreconcilable values, not because we sympathize with or detest him. We are instead awed by the performance.

The reader, during the moments of reading the tale (one could argue this even more confidently for the listener to the oral recitation),[10] is caught up in the spirit or pattern of rhetorical effects. While being mentally rushed along by the closely-packed apostrophes, *exempla,* and sales pitches poured out by the narrator, we can only admire or perhaps wonder at the temerity of the Pardoner. We cannot stop to analyze him psychologically or puzzle over irrational or eccentric behavior. It is only with reflection, when we try to abstract a plot outline or tie together the multi-colored threads of his personality, that we even think of the questions suggested at the start of his essay.

Instead, readers should consider the *Pardoner's Tale* as a forceful expression of a complex human reaction or feeling relevant to readers of all ages. To some degree, all of us are guilty of the same ironic contradictions in practice with regard to our ideals or religious beliefs, whatever they are. Or, if that seems too strong, we at least know that we see, rather obscurely, such contradictions in others about us. Such recognition explains why the tale affects us so strongly, providing such universal appeal. The contradictions we see in normal experience are never so sharply dramatized or communicated in such a full, coherent unity. In short, the Pardoner should be appreciated as an instrument for concrete, dramatic expression of such feeling, not as a character interesting for his own sake.

[10] Bertrand H. Bronson in *In Search of Chaucer* (Toronto, 1960), pp. 79–87, places special emphasis on the traditions of oral delivery for his argument against psychological realism in the *Pardoner's Tale.*

Chaucer's Pardoner, the Scriptural Eunuch, and the *Pardoner's Tale*

by Robert P. Miller

A recent article in *Speculum* suggested that Chaucer's Pardoner may best be understood in terms of Augustinian theology.[1] It is possible that the principles discussed there may be profitably elaborated. The intent of this paper is to indicate that the tradition of which St. Augustine was perhaps the most influential expositor provides more than a general climate of idea: specifically, that Scriptural imagery, utilized by Chaucer in the portrait and tale of the Pardoner, serves to illuminate quite precisely the nature of the man and the "moralite" of his sermon.

We are learning that the mediaeval author sought to build up the surface or *cortex* of his work in such a way as to indicate some particular *nucleus,* or inner meaning.[2] For this purpose he had at his command two main sources of material: the Book of Nature or God's Creation—the data of sense perception, and another Book—the Bible—which offered the unperceived data of revelation. Both "Books" provided the opportunity to achieve by study and interpretation a better knowledge of their Author. The Old Testament foreshadowed the "New Law" of charity under a series of types or figures, and was con-

[1] A. L. Kellogg, "An Augustinian Interpretation of Chaucer's Pardoner," *Speculum,* XXVI (1951), 465–481.

[2] Readers familiar with the recent work of Prof. D. W. Robertson, Jr., will recognize my indebtedness to his method of interpreting mediaeval vernacular poetry through its use of conventional Scriptural symbolism. For the distinction between *cortex* and *nucleus* see his "Some Medieval Literary Terminology, with Special Reference to Chrétien de Troyes," SP, XLVIII (1951), 669–692, esp. 671 ff. An interrelated series of specific Scriptural images is examined at length in his "The Doctrine of Charity in Mediaeval Literary Gardens," *Speculum,* XXVI (1951), 24–49. A full analysis of a mediaeval poem in accordance with these principles is found in *Piers Plowman and the Scriptural Tradition* (Princeton, 1951) by Professors Robertson and B. F. Huppé.

sequently to be reinterpreted in this light. Both the Bible and the Book of Nature provided a type of surface reality—a series of signs which, if properly understood, reflected the will and the law of God.

The *compaignye* created by Geoffrey Chaucer for the most famous fourteenth-century literary pilgrimage has been almost microscopically examined by the modern scholar in the effort to arrive at the most satisfactory understanding possible of the text of the *Canterbury Tales*. The characters are so firmly conceived that attempts have been made to identify the actual prototypes whom Chaucer may himself have known; and considerable study has been devoted to the various mediaeval sciences which provided details of psychological or physiognomical characteristics. It is surprising, however, to find scholarly effort directed so intensively upon what the mediaeval author called the *cortex* of his work, without an equally persistent effort to discover what *nucleus* might lie beneath. What we now call realism was of itself only a point of departure in a world where man's sensible experience consistently reflected the presence and nature of his Creator—where reality itself lay beneath the sign. The criterion of ulterior signification is, in fact, a hallmark of literature as a mode of expression. We expect the "cortex" to set forth a "nucleus" which is not denotable by scientific description. The reality of literature in any age may be said to lie beneath the sign, although the complexity of signification may not, perhaps, be as extensive or as arbitrary as that afforded the mediaeval artist by a highly developed system of conventional Scriptural symbolism.

Surface realism, however, even in the Middle Ages, was desirable insofar as it did not obscure the real issue of a particular work; and there is ample justification for historical study of the "realistic" details of mediaeval literature by which its inner sense is communicated to the reader. We have tended, nevertheless, to minimize the importance of the main source of mediaeval symbolic expression: that is, the Bible which, as the Word of God, provided, along with the Book of God's other works, the means for ulterior knowledge. Even if enigmatic, the words of the Bible could not be doubted, and here too, as with the Book of Nature, interpretation demanded insight. With respect to either, the letter killed, while the spirit gave life.

In his analysis of the Pardoner and his "secret" eunuchry, Professor Curry has adequately demonstrated that Chaucer's account is "scientifically correct." [3] But, although he approaches an inner equivalent for the detail he examines, Curry clarifies only the "letter" of this provocative characteristic. [4] It would be strange indeed if Chaucer had

[3] W. C. Curry, *Chaucer and the Medieval Sciences* (New York, 1926), 54–70. See p. 61.

[4] *Ibid.*, p. 64. See G. G. Sedgewick, "The Progress of Chaucer's Pardoner, 1880–1940," *MLQ*, I (1940), 435, 436.

intended his characters to be recognizable as particular living individuals, or as scientific phenomena, and nothing more. In this paper I wish first to indicate the literary purpose of the detail of eunuchry used in the description of the Pardoner—the *nucleus* beneath this element of the *cortex*. The detail may be shown to apply, not particularly to an individual *quaestor* of the House of Rouncevale, but to any pilgrim on his earthly pilgrimage. The Pardoner's "secret" may thus hold the secret of his literary existence. It will be my purpose to show how Chaucer, in making his Pardoner a eunuch, intended to expose and to stress the essential nature of this Canterbury pilgrim. It should be understood that this paper does not attempt to establish sources for idea or phraseology, except generally in Biblical context. For the present purpose it has been necessary to limit severely the associations connected with various Scriptural images, and citations of patristic writers have usually been minimized to offer an indicative selection of statements which may be found repeated in different ways elsewhere.

I

The last of all the pilgrims described in the General Prologue, the Pardoner is pictured as riding along singing a duet with that other "noble ecclesiaste," the Summoner:

> With hym ther rood a gentil PARDONER
> Of Rouncivale, his freend and his compeer,
> That streight was comen fro the court of Rome.
> Ful loude he soong "Com hider, love, to me!"
> This Somonour bar to hym a stif burdoun;
> Was nevere trompe of half so greet a soun.[5]
>
> (669-74)

These two compeers, whose business in theory is to increase and multiply the congregation of the faithful in the Church, are ironically singing a popular song of carnal, rather than spiritual, love—of cupidity (to use the conventional mediaeval distinction) rather than of charity.[6] Like January in his garden,[7] the Pardoner tries to put on a

---

[5] See A. L. Kellogg and L. A. Haselmayer, "Chaucer's Satire of the Pardoner," *PMLA*, LXVI (1951), 275-276 on the satiric juxtaposition of the Pardoner with the Summoner.

[6] Robinson notes, with disapproval, Gollancz's suggestion of a reflection of Cant. iv, 7-8. Here Christ the Bridegroom bids His Church to come forth to Him. What really matters is that Chaucer has his churchmen sing of "secular" love. It is worth noting that the old man, January (*MerchT*. 2144-2147) echoes the same verse in a similarly perverted manner. See Robertson, *Speculum*, XXVI, (1951), 45; and below, n. 28.

[7] *MerchT.*, 2025-2026.

gay and new exterior: with his hood folded in his wallet, "Hym
thoughte he rood al of the newe jet." Chaucer does not fail to note,
however, that, despite his "newe" appearance and the lecherous look
in his eye, this man is somewhat less than he seems.

> Swiche glarynge eyen hadde he as an hare . . .
> A voys he hadde as smal as hath a goot.
> No berd hadde he, ne nevere sholde have;
> As smothe it was as it were late shave.
> I trowe he were a geldyng or a mare.
>
> (688–91)

The images of the hare, goat and horse—all common symbols of
lechery—do not prevent notice that this man is also described as a
eunuch. In choosing this descriptive detail Chaucer may have had in
mind a concept used in several Biblical texts and dealt with by many
patristic commentators. In such terms the rather extraordinary detail
of eunuchry may be shown not to be haphazard.

The symbol of the eunuch receives noteworthy Scriptural treatment
in three separate texts: Deuteronomy xxiii. 1, Isaiah lvi. 3–5, and
Matthew xix. 12. They are sometimes considered independently in
Biblical commentaries, but more often the texts are referred to each
other for clarification and exposition. Thus Rupertus, in a very full
consideration of the prohibition of eunuchs under the Old Law, cites
all three texts:

> *Non intrabit eunuchus attritis vel amputatis testiculis et abscisso veretro
> in ecclesiam Domini.* In Isaia legimus: *Et non dicat Eunuchus: Ecce ego
> lignum aridum, quia haec dicit Dominus eunuchis: Si custodierint sab-
> bata mea, et egerint quae volui, et tenuerint foedus meum, dabo eis in
> domo mea, et in muris meis locum et nomen melius, a filiis et filiabus
> nomen sempiternum dabo eis quod non peribit (Isa.* lvi). Ergone sic sibi
> contraria sunt lex et prophetae, ut dicat lex, *non intrabit eunuchus in
> ecclesiam Domini,* dicat econtra Dominus in propheta: *Dabo eunuchus
> locum in domo mea, et in muris meis?* Quae est enim domus, aut qui
> muri Domini, nisi ecclesia Domini? Sed profecto intellectus eunuchi non
> idem hic est et illic. Illic enim in littera, hic autem in spiritu eunuchus
> intelligendus est, quia spiritualis est. Quapropter jam ipsas eunuchorum
> enumeremus species. In Evangelio Dominus dicit: *Sunt eunuchi qui sic
> nati sunt; et sunt eunuchi qui ab hominibus facti sunt; et sunt eunuchi
> qui se castraverunt propter regnum caelorum (Matth.* xix). Haec tertia
> eunuchizatio, sive castratio, quia non ferro abscissionis, sed proposito fit
> castitatis, magis quidem spiritualis est, verumtamen non omnino, quia
> manifestus in carne caelibatus est. Et hi procul dubio laudabiles sunt
> eunuchi, quibus, juxta prophetam praedictum, dat Dominus *locum in
> domo sua, et in muris suis* nomenque melius a filiis et filiabus.[8]

[8] Rupertus Tuitiensis, *De Trinitate et operibus ejus. In Deuteronomia,* I, xxii
(*PL,* CLXVII, col. 941–942). Rupertus' commentary is quoted as it contains a very clear
development of these conventional ideas.

["A eunuch, with his testicles impaired or amputated, and his privates removed, shall not enter the Lord's church." We read in Isaiah: "Neither let the eunuch say: 'Behold, I am a dry tree,' for the Lord has said to eunuchs: 'If they have kept my sabbaths and done the things I wanted and taken hold of my covenant, I will give them in my house and within my walls a place and a better name than sons and daughters, an eternal name that shall not perish' " (Isa. lvi). So, are not the law and the prophets thus at odds, since the law says: "A eunuch shall not enter into the Lord's church," whereas the Lord says, through His prophet: "I will give to eunuchs a place in my house and within my walls"? For what is the house, or what the walls of the Lord, if not His church? But actually the meaning of the word eunuch is not the same in these two places. For in the former the eunuch is to be understood as one literally, but in the latter, spiritually, because he is a spiritual one. So, let us, at this point, list the types of eunuchs. In the Gospel the Lord says: "There are eunuchs who were born such, there are man-made eunuchs, and there are eunuchs who have castrated themselves for the sake of the kingdom of heaven" (Matth. xix). This third type of eunuchization or castration, which happens not through cutting with iron, but by the intention of chastity, is even more a spiritual one, though not entirely, because celibacy is manifested through the flesh. And these are without doubt the praiseworthy eunuchs, those to whom, it has been predicted according to the prophet, the Lord will give "a place in His house and in His walls" and a name better than sons and daughters.]

The eunuch according to the Old Law is prohibited from entering the church of the Lord; under the New Law he is given a place within its walls. Rupertus' preliminary distinction between two types of eunuchry is according to the conventional principle that the Old Law was literal, while the New was to be understood according to the spirit. The "spiritual eunuchs" are those who, by an act of will, lead the life of chastity for the sake of the kingdom of heaven. He continues with an interpretation of the letter of the Old Law:

Horum omnium generum de nullo veraciter dicas, quia non ingreditur ecclesiam Domini, nisi quod sacros tantum altaris honores auctoritas canonica truncatis vel abscissis interdicit. Quapropter quaerendum adhuc est qualis sit ille eunuchus, qui non ingrediatur ecclesiam Domini. Quaerentibus hoc illis quoque illud sese offert quod alibi dictum est: *Maledictus omnis qui non fecit semen in Israel* [*Deut.* vii. 14]. Neutrum quippe sine altero recte intelligi potest, quia videlicet verba quidem diversa, sensus tamen idem est. Igitur eunuchus qui non ingrediatur in ecclesiam Domini, et non faciens semen in Israel, qui et idcirco maledictus esse debeat, quia semen non fecerit in Israel, ille est, qui cum possit verbo aedificare proximum, mutus incedit, vel cum bona et utilia noverit, otiosa magis et vana diligit. Hic illi oppositus est qui se castravit propter regnum coelorum, quia videlicet quantum ille laudabilis est, eo quod facultatem habens naturalem seminandi filios, carnis continens est propter regnum coelorum, scilicet ut vacare possit orationi, et juxta

apostolicum consilium tantum sollicitus sit quae sunt Domini; tantum
hic detestabilis est, eo quod commissum habens talentum verbi Dei, quo
ad aedificationem multorum bene possit operari et utiliter negotiari,
vacat otio, et acceptam indigne gratiam negligit.

[You could not say truly of any one of all these types that he does not
enter the church of the Lord, except in that canonical precept forbids to
the mutilated and the maimed only the holy duties of the altar. And
so we must ask now what sort of eunuch it is who may not enter the
church of the Lord. To askers of this question another thing presents
itself, which is said elsewhere: "Cursed be he who does not produce seed
in Israel" (Deut. vii. 14). Certainly neither saying can be understood
aright without the other for, obviously, though the words be different
the sense is nevertheless the same. Therefore, the eunuch who may not
enter the church of the Lord, and does not produce seed in Israel—and
for that reason ought to be cursed—is that man who, though able to
edify his neighbor by his words, goes about silent, or he who, though
he knows the good and profitable, chooses the idle and empty. Opposed
to him is the man who castrates himself for the sake of the kingdom of
heaven; for obviously he is so praiseworthy precisely because, though he
possesses the natural power of begetting children, he is continent as regards the flesh for the sake of the kingdom of heaven, which is to say,
so that he might be free for prayer and, according to apostolic intention,
be only interested in the things of the Lord. That other is so detestable
precisely because, though having the responsibility of the word of God
entrusted to him, whereby he might be capable of good works and fruitful tasks for the edification of many, he has time for idleness and
meanly ignores available grace.]

This exposition may be valuable for an understanding of Chaucer's
use of the idea of eunuchry in his description of the Pardoner. By
following the standard exegetical principle of interpreting the letter
of the Old Law in terms of the spirit of the New, Rupertus arrives,
in effect, at a triple distinction among varieties of eunuchry equivalent
to the statement in Matthew. Of the three types of eunuchry, then, one
is literal (Deuteronomy according to the letter, and the *eunuchi qui
nati sunt* of Matthew), and two are spiritual. Besides eunuchry
thought of as voluntary chastity, we are presented with another figurative type (Matthew's second) which Rupertus characterizes as *detestabilis,* the antithesis of the laudable spiritual eunuchry—an opposition
emphasized in the parallel grammatical construction of his discussion.
This eunuchry is also the result of an act of will, but of an opposite
act in that this man, in full knowledge of the *bona et utilia,* chooses
the worse part: the *otiosa . . . et vana.* This man, possessing the
ability to inform his neighbor, remains silent; knowing the value of
good works, he chooses idleness. Instead of cutting himself off from
evil works,[9] he cuts himself off from good works. He refuses offered

[9] Herveus, *Commentarii in Isaiam,* VII, lvi (*PL,* CLXXXI, col. 512): "Eunuchi, sunt
qui pressis motibus carnis effectum in se pravi operis excidunt." [Eunuchs are

grace. In short, he is the presumptuous man who, by *his* act of will, commits the unpardonable sin, not for the sake of, but in despite of, the kingdom of heaven. He holds a position in Babylon exactly equivalent to that held by his opposite in Jerusalem. Other commentators reflect a similar conception, though usually in less detail.

In the light of the division in Matthew and the exegetes, the "natural eunuch," or the *eunuchus ex nativitate,* treated by Professor Curry in his discussion of the Pardoner is not, for the purpose of significant characterization, as pertinent as the opposition between the two states of spiritual eunuchry. We need not assume from Chaucer's text that the character described was a eunuch from birth. Indeed, even if we recognize the exactness of the description, literary justification of this usage demands the shift to its spiritual analogy. The second class distinguished in Matthew is, in fact, often considered as both literal and spiritual eunuchry.[10]

Besides the significant treatment of the idea by Rupertus, it is not difficult to find equally suggestive statements in other places. The *Glossa Ordinaria* itself reflects the opposition already noted. In the second class of eunuchs it places those false religious who deceptively put on the guise of religion, but in reality are not chaste: the wolves in sheep's clothing. "Inter hos computantur etiam hic qui specie religionis simulant castitatem." [11] [Among those are included here people who counterfeit chastity with the appearance of religion.] Consonant with these remarks is also the opposition by Paschasius Radbertus between the *eunuchus Dei* and the *eunuchus non Dei.*[12] Rabanus Maurus gives a most significant account of the *eunuchi qui facti sunt:*

> Possumus et aliter dicere, eunuchi sunt ex matris utero qui sunt frigidioris naturae, nec libidinem appetentes, et aliqui ab hominibus fiunt quos aut philosophi faciunt, aut propter idolorum cultum emolliuntur in feminas, vel persuasione haeretica simulant charitatem, ut mentiantur religionis veritatem; sed nullus eorum consequitur regnum coelorum, nisi qui se propter Christum castraverit.[13]

> [We can also mention that there are eunuchs from birth, who are of a frigid nature, as they are not interested in sexual desire; also some are man-made, either by philosophies, or through idolatrous worship they soften into women, or through a heretical conviction simulate chastity in order to misrepresent the truth of religion; but not one of them

---

those who, by checking the impulses of the flesh, cut off the effects of evil works upon themselves.]

[10] E.g., by Rupertus, *loc. cit.; Glossa Ordinaria (PL,* cxiv, col. 148); Rabanus Maurus, *Commentarii in Matthaeum (PL,* cvii, col. 1018–1019).

[11] To Matth. xix, 12 *(PL,* cxiv, vol. 148). Cp. *Pard. prol.* 421–422.

[12] *Expositio in Matthaeum,* ix, xix *(PL,* cxx, col. 654–656).

[13] *Op. cit., PL,* cvii, col. 1019.

follows the kingdom of heaven except the one who castrates himself for Christ.]

The *eunuchus non Dei*—the perverted, or perverse, churchman—is he who, according to Deuteronomic law, *non intrabit in ecclesiam Domini.* Commentaries on Deuteronomy xxiii, 1 also describe this type of eunuchry with clarity. The *Glossa Ordinaria* explains the prohibition thus: "*Non intrabit.* Omnes qui molliter vivunt, nec virile opus perficiunt, non possunt permanere in congregatione sanctorum nec digni sunt introitu regni coelorum, quod violentiam patitur, et violenti diripiunt illud." [14] [*Shall not enter.* All who live luxuriously and do not do their manly duties cannot remain in the body of saints, nor are they worthy of entrance into the kingdom of heaven, which suffers violence, and the violent bear it away.] The false eunuch is the man who lives at ease (*vacat otio,* in Rupertus' words), and does not carry out "manly" works. That is to say, he is sterile in good works, impotent to produce spiritual fruit. Bruno Astensis is more specific yet: "Per hoc enim significatur, quod in coelestem patriam nullus intrabit, qui bonorum operorum sterilis, spiritualis generationis et fecunditatis instrumenta non habuit." [15] [For this is meant, that no one shall enter his heavenly homeland who is sterile in good works and does not have the means of spiritual generation and fecundity.] This eunuch might truly cry, "Ecce ego lignum aridum" [16] [Behold, I am a dry tree].

We may carry the metaphor one step farther. The spiritual fruits, or progeny, which the upright produce are, traditionally, as Bruno suggests, virtues or good works. St. Augustine refers several times to the analogy by which good works represent spiritual offspring. "Quid est, filios tuos? Opera tua quae hic agis. Qui sunt filii filiorum? Fructus operum tuorum. Facis eleemosynas, filii tui sunt: propter eleemosynas

---

[14] *PL,* CXIII, col. 477. Bede, *In Pentateuchum commentarii—Deuteronomium (PL,* XCI, col. 391), and Rabanus Maurus, *Enarratio super Deuteronomium,* III, vii (*PL,* CVIII, col. 929) make the same statement almost verbatim.

[15] *Expositio in Deuteronomium (PL,* CLXIV, col. 526).

[16] See Herveus, *op. cit.,* col. 511–512: "Et hujusmodi eunuchis prohibetur dicere: *Ecce ego lignum aridum,* id est homo infructuosus, quia non de carnali, sed de spirituali fecunditate debet cogitare." [And it is prohibited to eunuchs to speak in this way: "Behold, I am a dry tree," that is, a sterile man, because it is not of fleshly but of spiritual fertility that he ought to think.] Haymo, *Commentarius in Isaiam,* III, lvi (*PL,* CXVI, col. 1007): "Non abscidendo sibi virilia, sed luxuriam refrenando. . . . Ibi enim non de semine procreationis dicitur, sed de semine bonae operationis, . . . quia non separabuntur a gloria electorum, si semen spirituale hic, id est opus bonum fecerint: sed coronam et bravium virginitatis a Domino recipient." [Not by cutting off the male members but by holding extravagant living in check. . . . For the seed of procreation is not spoken of there but the seed of good works, . . . because they will not be kept from the glory of the elect if they produce spiritual seed, that is, good works. On the contrary, they will receive the crown and prize of virginity from the Lord.]

accipis vitam acternam, filii filiorum tuorum sunt." [17] [What are they, your sons? They are the works which you do here. Who are the sons of your sons? The fruits of your works. If you give alms, they are your sons. On account of giving alms, you receive eternal life, the sons of your sons.] For this idea the most obvious Scriptural basis is Genesis, i, 28, in which the Lord, having created man in His own image, male and female, "Benedixitque illis, et ait: Crescite et multiplicamini, et replete terram et subjicite eam" [And he blessed them, and said: "Increase and multiply and fill the earth and subdue it]. This benediction is usually distinguished from that given the beasts (Gen. i, 22) which was a precept for physical multiplication only. While man was granted the necessity of such increase, his blessing referred also to the soul by which he was superior to the beasts. For man, then, the precept instituted the state of honorable marriage,[18] but further prescribed for the soul the multiplication of virtues by spiritual fertility.[19] Common also is the interpretation according to which man is thus commanded to "increase and multiply" the congregation of the faithful that the number of the elect might be fulfilled: ". . . suavius est hoc sentire quod si homo non peccaset, tam multa tamque vitiosa progenies de carne ejus non pullulasset, sed solum praedictae benedictionis fructum, id est, electos omnes et solos germinasset, non more jumentorum ruendo in libidinem, sed rationis imperio per mundam carnis naturam aedificando praedestinatam coeli progeniem." [20] [It is more pleasant to consider that if man had not sinned so many corrupt offspring of his flesh would not have come forth, but only the fruit of the foretold blessing—that is, he would have produced all the elect and only them, not in uncontrolled desire

---

[17] *Enarratio in Psalmum CXXVIII*[:6] (*PL*, xxxvii, col. 1688). See also, e.g., *PL*, xxxvii, col. 1724; *PL*, xlii, col. 1004; above, n. 16.

[18] See, e.g., Rabanus Maurus, *Commentarii in Genesim* (*PL*, cvii, col. 458–459; 461–462); Peter Comestor, *Historia Scholastica, Liber Genesis*, x (*PL*, cxcviii, col. 1064); Angelomus, *Commentarius in Genesim* (*PL*, cxv, col. 128); *Commentarii in Genesim*, attrib. St. Eucherius (*PL*, i, col. 901); etc.

[19] "Fecunditas animae" in the *Commentarii in Genesim*, attrib. St Eucherius, *loc. cit.*, which interprets *implete terram:* "Terram intelligunt carnem, quam implet anima, et dominatur, cum in virtute multiplicatur." ['Earth' they understand as 'flesh,' which, when it is increased in virtue, the spirit fills and controls.] Thus also Angelomus, *loc. cit.*, states: "Salva historiale narratione, potest referri ad fecunditatem animae, *crescite*, id est, multiplicamini augmentando virtutes, et *replete terram,* sub carnis virtutibus fecunditate, et subjicite spiritui, et dominamini bestiis, hoc est motibus, quos similes bestiis, per temperantiam." [Without violation of the historical narrative, it is possible for 'increase' to refer to the fecundity of the spirit—that is, you are increased by the augmentation of virtues—and 'fill the earth,' to be fruitful through the virtues of the flesh, subject it to the spirit, and subdue the beasts, namely the impulses which are like those of beasts, through moderation.] See also Rabanus Maurus, *Commentarii in Genesim* (*PL*, cvii, col. 468).

[20] Rupertus, *op. cit., In Genesim*, ii, ix (*PL*, clxvii, col. 254).

like beasts of burden but under the sway of reason through the clean nature of the flesh, building up the predestined progeny of heaven.] With respect to the concept of spiritual "multiplication" reference is also frequently made to Psalm lxxxvii. 3: "Multiplicabis me in anima mea, virtute." [21] [You will increase me in my spirit, in virtue.] By increase in good works and multiplication in virtues, or by augmenting the number of the faithful, the *eunuchus Dei* may properly be said to be fecund. "Porro in tertio [eunuchizatio] spes regni coelestis fide genita propagatur in charitate, qua multos generare filios magis quam carne creditur." [22] [Moreover, in the third type of eunuchry, where faith has been engendered, hope for the kingdom of heaven is propagated through charity, by which it is believed to beget many children, more than by the flesh.] It is in just such spiritual multiplication that the *eunuchus non Dei* is sterile, a *lignum aridum*. As Rupertus said, he deliberately refuses to perform good works, and wilfully turns away from virtue.

II

If we look at Chaucer's Pardoner in terms of the Christian concept of eunuchry, both the utility of the image and the true character of this "noble ecclesiaste" are illuminated. According to these terms we should indeed expect him to be a eunuch. As a man in orders, he should be one of those "qui seipsos sua sponte castraverunt propter regnum coelorum . . . permanentes in castitate" [23] [who castrate themselves of their own free will for the sake of the kingdom of heaven . . . remaining chaste throughout]. That is, the ecclesiastic is figuratively supposed to be the third type of eunuch distinguished in Matthew—one who by his own will has cut himself off from temporal pleasures, "non ferro . . . sed totus gladio Spiritus sancti praecisus, quod est verbum Dei: atque circumcisus intus forisve, ne ulla in eo prurigo concupiscentiarum praevaleat" [24] [not with iron . . . but separated off entire by the sword of the Holy Spirit, that is, the word of God, and cut off on all sides within and without, lest any provocations to concupiscence get the upper hand in him]. Castration or circumcision by the word of God is equivalent to cutting away the *vetus homo* that the *novus homo* might live: [25] this eunuch's "voluntas," says Radbertus, is "nova secundum Spiritum sanctum procreata" [26] [a new will, begotten according to the Holy Spirit].

[21] See St. Augustine's exposition (*PL*, xxxvii, col. 1778).
[22] Radbertus, *op. cit.* (*PL*, cxx, col. 655).
[23] *Ibid.*, col. 654.
[24] *Ibid.*, col. 654–655.
[25] See Rom. vi, 6–11; Col. iii, 7–10; Eph. iv, 22–23. This associated concept is treated more fully below.
[26] *Op. cit.*, col. 655.

The Pardoner, according to his own boast, is by no means a eunuch in this sense. The opposite, however, implicit in the developed Christian concept of eunuchry, provides a sense quite appropriate to the man as he presents himself in his prologue and tale; and this opposition itself implies a biting and bitter satire directed at the type of churchman he represents. It is evident that by *his* act of will he has cut himself off from virtue and good works, and that this act has been performed, not "amore Christi," [27] that is, through charity, but through its antithesis, *cupiditas.* The animal symbols of lechery with which he is associated immediately suggest that, although he is perhaps physically frustrated, the inner man hardly "abides in chastity." If the *eunuchus Dei* is the *novus homo* of Scripture, the Pardoner, having cut away this possibility, lives impenitently the life of the *vetus homo.*

Upon such oppositions, basic to Scriptural imagery and exegesis, the portrait of the Pardoner is developed by Chaucer. The song of cupidity with which he is introduced, for example, strongly suggests the *vetus canticum* sung by the *vetus homo,* itself the reverse of the *canticum novum* which the new man sings: "vetus homo canticum vetus cantare potest, non novum. Ut autem cantet canticum novum, sit novus homo." [28] [The old man can sing the old song, not the new. However, so that he might sing the new song, let him be a new man.]

More definite, however, is the comparison provided between the Pardoner and the parson whom he is said to gull with his false relics.

> But with thise relikes, whan that he fond
> A povre person dwellynge upon lond,
> Upon a day he gat hym moore moneye
> Than that the person gat in monthes tweye;
> And thus, with feyned flaterye and japes,
> He made the person and the peple his apes.
>
> (701–6)

The comparison seems to be purposefully introduced in order to play off the character of the Pardoner against that of the "povre PERSOUN OF THE TOUN" who yet was rich "of hooly thought and werk"—that is, of virtue and good deeds, the spiritual progeny of the true eunuch. The Parson, we recall, "also a lerned man, a clerk, That Cristes gospel *trewely wolde preche,*" [29] preaches in churches for mo-

---

[27] *Ibid.*

[28] St Augustine, *Sermo IX: de decem chordis* (PL, xxxviii, col. 81).

[29] *Gen. Prol.,* 479–481, italics mine. The Pardoner, in what H. R. Patch called "Chaucer's most unsparing couplet in all his works" (*On Rereading Chaucer* [Cambridge, Mass., 1939], p. 164), says: "Thus spitte I out my venym under hewe Of hoolynesse, to *semen* hooly and *trewe.*" "Truth" is also "loaded" as a Christian term. Christ calls himself Truth (John xiv. 6). Compare Chaucer's *Balade de Bon Conseyl (Truth).* The opposite is falseness, *mendacium* (see below, n. 46).

tives other than *cupiditas;* his interest, as it should be, is in increasing
and multiplying the congregation of the faithful:

> To drawen folk to hevene by fairnesse,
> By good ensample, this was his bisynesse.[30]   (519–20)

He is a shepherd, not a mercenary. Of all these traits the Pardoner
possesses the opposite, by his own rather proud admission. The Parson
who with his "brother" may be said to live in "parfit charitee," like
the true eunuch who has devoted his life to others *propter regnum
coelorum* and thus multiplies spiritually, is a perfect foil to the
Pardoner. By spiritual standards the best of all the pilgrims, he is
ironically compared with one who, in his perfect cupidity, is possibly
the worst of the lot.

The Pardoner does better the Parson in one respect: "he gat hym
moore moneye." But to do this he subverts the Parson and all that he
stands for. The analogy of his "Com hider, love," in Church, is the
"offertorie," the purpose of which he reverses by applying it to his own
benefit rather than to God's. Like the song he sings with the Summoner,
this is the *vetus canticum* of cupidity rather than the *canticum novum*
of charity. The increase of his money is typical of the Pardoner's *multiplicatio.* Sterile in the spiritual multiplication of heavenly treasure,
he lays up his treasure on earth. Since Deuteronomy stated that such
eunuchs shall not enter *in ecclesiam Domini,* it is ironic that the
Pardoner is said to conduct most of his business "in chirches." [31] Here
he advertises his own variety of multiplications with a calculated
propaganda. The goodman who uses his "sholdre-boon, Which that
was of a hooly Jewes sheep," with the proper magic ritual, "As thilke
hooly Jew our eldres taughte," (suggestive of the Old Law) will find
"His beestes and his stoor *shal multiplye.*" His marvelous mitten,
equally useful to the man who wishes to get ahead in the world, will
provide "*multiplying* of his grayn." [32] The formula here is the offering
of "pens, or elles grotes."

The Pardoner thus makes of the Church a kind of medicine show,
and will promise to multiply earthly and material things, a function
singularly appropriate to the particular type of sterility he represents.

> Multis modis multiplicatio intelligi potest. Est multiplicatio terrenae
> generationis, secundum primam naturae nostrae benedictionem. . . .
> Et ista plane multiplicatio fructuosa est, et non venit nisi de benedic-
> tione Domini. Jam quid dicam de aliis multiplicationibus. Multiplicatus

---

[30] And see his prologue, 49–51.

[31] *Gen. Prol.* 707 states: "He was *in chirche* a noble ecclesiaste." The first line of
the Pardoner's prologue runs: "'Lordynges,' quod he, 'in chirches whan I preche'"
(329; cf. 378).

[32] In this and the previous quotation, italics mine.

est ille auro, ille argento, ille pecore, ille familia, ille possessionibus, ille his omnibus. Multae sunt terrenae multiplicationes. . . . Etenim curis homines in anima multiplicantur. Multiplicatus videtur in anima, in quo etiam multiplicata sunt vitia. Ille tantummodo luxuriosus; iste et avarus, et superbus, et luxuriosis: multiplicatus est in anima sua, sed malo suo. Multiplicatio ista egestatis est, non ubertatis.[33]

['Increase' can be understood in many ways. There is increase with respect to earthly generation, according to the first blessing upon our nature. . . . And that sort of increase is clearly a fruitful one and does not come without the blessing of the Lord. But now, what am I to say of other increases? One man increases his gold, one his silver, one his flock, one his family, one his possessions, one all these things. Many are the earthly increases. . . . And yet men are increased by their cares in spirit. One seems increased in spirit in whom, indeed, are multiplied his vices. One is only increased in dissolute living; another is avaricious, and proud, and dissolute: he is increased in his spirit, but by his evil. Such an increase is one of poverty, not of abundance.]

Multiplicationes terrenae, the increase of earthly treasure, are those at which the spiritually sterile excel. The Pardoner in this activity uses his "relikes" to turn the mind of the goodman not to God through charity, but to his personal material wealth through cupidity: a reversal insidiously perverse with regard to his victim's eternal well-being. The increase he offers (and even this is "feyned") is that of the *vetus homo*—the opposite of the multiplyings of the *novus homo*. So far as the latter are concerned, the Pardoner is wilfully a sterile man; and it is probable that this is what Chaucer alludes to when he remarks, "I trow he were a gelding or a mare," a gelding, that is, "qui bonorum operum sterilis, spiritualis generationis et fecunditatis instrumenta non habuit" [who is sterile of good works and does not have the means of spiritual generation and fecundity]; and a mare, that is, one of those who "propter idolorum cultum emolliuntur in feminas" [through idolatrous worship soften into women].

If the Pardoner may be analyzed in terms of the *eunuchus non Dei,* his nature and status among the pilgrims of the *Canterbury Tales* may be further clarified in terms of its equivalent—the *vetus homo.* The term "Old Man" is Paul's (cf. Col. iii, 1–10; Eph. iv, 17–24; Rom. vi, 1 ff.), who also calls him the "body of sin." As an aspect of the

---

[33] St. Augustine, *Enarratio in Psalmum CXXXVII*[:3] (*PL,* xxxvii, col. 1778). Compare his *Enarratio in Psalmum IV*[:8] (*PL,* xxxvi, col. 82): "Non enim multiplicatio semper ubertatem significat, et non plerumque exiguitatem: cum dedita temporalibus voluptatibus anima semper exardescit cupiditate, nec satiari potest, et multiplici atque aerumnosa cogitatione distenta, simplex bonum videre non sinitur." [For 'increase' does not always signify abundance, and occasionally it signifies poverty: for when the spirit is given over to temporal pleasures it is always inflamed with avarice, nor can it be satisfied, and, distended with manifold troublesome considerations, it is not granted a view of the simple good.]

nature of man, the *vetus homo* represents the flesh and its manifold
lusts, opposed to the *novus homo:* that is, the spirit and reason, by
which these are subdued.[34] In terms of the Biblical history of man,
the Old Man, in any human being, is the image of fallen Adam, unregenerate in accepted grace and unredeemed by Christ, Who is called
the "New Man." [35] As the result of original sin, all men are said to be
born in the image of the *vetus Adam.* By baptism, however, we are
said to die to sin and to be reborn in the image of Christ; and he who
adopts this image is termed the New Man (sometimes the Young Man).
As Christ's flesh was crucified and buried that the Old Law might be
overthrown, so should the *vetus homo,* or the flesh, be crucified and
buried, first in baptism (Rom. vi, 4–6) and later in penance, by a similar free act of will. Through this death man achieves life under the
New Law, as the *eunuchus Dei,* by an analogous act, achieves spiritual
potency.

This brief account of the *vetus homo* is intended to suggest a common cluster of ideas also utilized by Chaucer in his description of the
Pardoner. Although this man thinks he deceives his fellows by putting
on external "newness," his "newe jet" does not completely disguise the
Old Man, sterile in charitable works, beneath.[36] There is irony also in
his plea to another false preacher:

> "Now, dame," quod he, "by God and by seint John!
> Ye been a noble prechour in this cas.
> I was aboute to wedde a wyf; allas!
> What sholde I bye it on my flessh so deere?
> Yet hadde I levere wedde no wyf to-yeere!"
>
> (III.164–68)

> . . . .
> "Telle forth youre tale, spareth for no man,
> And teche *us yonge men* of youre praktike" [37]
>
> (III.186–87)

[34] Equivalent terms are the "exterior man" and the "animal man," which likewise
have their opposites, the "interior man" and the "rational man." A more complete
understanding of this familiar concept may be gained from the popular commentaries upon the Biblical texts cited. It is also a staple of sermon literature.

[35] The *vetus homo* is often called the *vetus Adam;* Christ the *novus Adam.*

[36] In fact, as elsewhere, by Scriptural echo Chaucer calls our attention to the
reality. In the Latin of Eph. vii, 24, the term is *"induite* novum hominem," literally
used with reference to putting on articles of dress or ornament. The Pardoner has
also, ironically, "put off" his hood, which may be thought of as symbolizing the
New Man (and in any case his proper ecclesiastical office). The hood of the Austin
Canon symbolized death to the vanities of the world (see M. P. Hamilton, "The
Credentials of Chaucer's Pardoner," *JEGP,* XL [1941], 63.)

[37] Italics mine. The "marriage" of the ecclesiastic is properly to the Church, and
involves penance of the flesh, by which the Old Man is "put off"—an ironic analogy
perhaps implied in the Pardoner's reservations regarding marriage. The seeming

That in his perfect cupidity he typifies the *vetus homo* (an identification strengthened by verbal hints) would have sufficiently condemned the Pardoner in the more perceptive minds of Chaucer's audience. What is worse, the man knows and freely admits the evil of his character. And worse yet, besides knowing the evil of cupidity and still practicing it, he is proud, even boastful, of his abilities. Like the "detestable" eunuch described by Rupertus, he is one "qui cum possit aedificare proximum, mutus incedit, vel cum bona et utilia noverit, otiosa magis et vana diligit" [who, though able to edify his neighbor by his words, goes about silent, or he who, though he knows the good and profitable, chooses the idle and empty]. Acting out of neither ignorance nor frailty, he is recognizable as the man impenitent in sin. Thus there is no hesitation in the confession of his prologue:

> But shortly myn entente I wol devyse;
> I preche of no thing but for coveityse.
> Therfore my theme is yet, and evere was,
> *Radix malorum est Cupiditas.*
> Thus can I preche agayn that same vice
> Which that I use, and that is avarice.[38]

> (423–28)

It is not difficult to recognize the theological type after which the Pardoner is figured. It is a type of sinner on which behavioristic sympathy is wasted (for the Pardoner is himself responsible for his figurative eunuchry). His eunuchry, his *vetustas,* and his pride, would easily have identified him as a man sinning vigorously against the Holy Ghost.

Presumption, or *peccatum in Spiritum sanctum,* is the one sin which is irremissible, since it involves the refusal of grace. St Augustine

inconsistency in the ecclesiastical status of the Pardoner (see Robinson, *ed. cit.,* p. 835, n. 416) may be only the result of such a double sense of his words. We are not prevented from thinking of him, of course, here as elsewhere, as attempting to disguise his eunuchry. The analogous disguise for the spiritual eunuchry under discussion is, however, the figurative marriage to the Church for the purpose of spiritual generation. The Pardoner is certainly one who, alas, never quite entered into this contract. There is probably more than "jocularity" involved here.

The "praktike" of the Wife of Bath is elsewhere described as the "olde daunce" (i.e. of cupidity), marriage to the flesh. The special characteristics of the Wife implied here will be discussed in another place. The "yonge men" with whom the Pardoner ironically classes himself, may be intended as the opposite of *veteres homines,* a fitting self-attribution by a master of duplicity. The term reappears suggestively to describe the "yonge folk" whom he treats in his tale (see lines 463, 758).

[38] It should be noted that Faux-Semblant, disguised as a friar, makes a similar false confession in the *Roman de la Rose* (see D. S. Fansler, *Chaucer and the Roman de la Rose* [New York, 1914], p. 162 ff.). Confession is said to be false if unaccompanied by contrition (see below, n. 45). Prof. B. F. Huppé is preparing an article on the dramatic significance of the Pardoner's presumption.

stressed final impenitence as the irremissible sin, for God is said not
to pardon where penitence is absent.[39] This sin is usually described in
terms of malice, the opposite or absence of charity. The less serious
sin against the Father arises through frailty (absence of power), and
that against the Son through ignorance (absence of wisdom).[40] Impenitence, or other aspects of this sin, are absolutely opposed to the remis-
sion of sins which is appropriated to the Holy Ghost.[41] It refuses
proffered grace without which there can be no pardon.[42] The grace
of the Holy Ghost precedes contrition, the first requisite of penitence,
as the Pardoner knows. Of the last requisite, penance, he sells partial
indulgence.[43]

Again the contrast with the Parson, whose tale is a penitential man-
ual, is evident. According to their offices, both the Pardoner and the
Parson are *media* through which grace may be brought to the faithful;[44] but the Pardoner, like Rupertus' *eunuchus detestabilis*, "ac-

---

[39] See, e.g., *Epistolae ad Romanos, inchoata expositio (PL*, xxxv, col. 2097). Peter
Lombard's standard discussion of the *peccatum in Spiritum sanctum* is in the
Sententiae, ii, dist. xliii. The text I use is that printed in the Quaracchi edition of
the works of St Bonaventura (Vol. ii, 1885). He treats Augustine's position on
p. 980a.

[40] See Lombard, *op. cit.*, p. 981b. The Pardoner says he sometimes preaches out
of malice, or "hate," for revenge (*Pard. prol.* 412 ff.). He may again be contrasted
with the Parson.

[41] Lombard, *op. cit.*, p. 980a: "Recte ergo in Spiritum sanctum delinquere dicun-
tur, qui sua malitia Dei bonitatem superare putant, et ideo poenitentiam non assu-
munt, et qui iniquitati tam pertinaci mente inhaerent, ut eam nunquam relinquere
proponant et ad bonitatem Spiritus sancti nunquam redire, patientia Dei abutentes
et de misericordia Dei nimis praesumentes." [Rightly therefore are they said to
transgress against the Holy Spirit who think to overcome the goodness of God by
their own evil, and who therefore are not repentant, and who persist in iniquity
so obstinately that they never intend to relinquish it, nor ever to return to the
goodness of the Holy Spirit in their abuse of the patience of God and their excessive
presumption upon His mercy.]

[42] St Augustine, *De sermone Domini in monte*, i (*PL*, xxxiv, col. 1267): "Et hoc est
fortasse peccare in Spiritum sanctum, id est, per malitiam et invidiam, fraternam
oppugnare charitatem post acceptam gratiam Spiritus sancti, quod peccatum Dominus neque hic, neque in futuro saeculo dimitti dicit." [This is also, perhaps, a sin
against the Holy Spirit, namely, through malice and envy to resist brotherly
charity after the proffered grace of the Holy Spirit, a sin which, the Lord says, is
neither now nor in future ages to be ignored.]

[43] Technically, the Pardoner receives a free gift of alms, itself effective as penance
(cf. Kellogg and Haselmeyer, *op. cit.*, p. 252). According to the rule of opposites,
almsgiving is usually specified for the sin of *coveitise*. It is impossible, within the
limits of this article, to elaborate the full irony of the situation. The Pardoner's
false confession—perversion of the second requisite in penitence; the full significance
of his refusal to "bye it on [his] flessh so deere," or of his own impenitence in relation to his official duties; his character and activities in the light of the theology of
indulgence and of preaching—all deserve investigation and can only be suggested
here.

[44] See Dom Jean Leclercq, "Le Magistère du Prédicateur au XIIIᵉ Siècle," *Archives
d'Histoire Doctrinale et Littéraire du Moyen Age* (1946), 108–115, esp. 109.

ceptam indigne gratiam negligit" [meanly ignores available grace]. A type of the impenitent man, the Pardoner accumulates temporal wealth by making a mockery of penitence and pardon. Like the eunuchs described by Rabanus Maurus, who "persuasione haeretica simulant charitatem, ut mentiantur religionis veritatem" [through a heretical conviction simulate chastity in order to misrepresent the truth of religion], he knowingly perverts the function of his office. According to St Augustine, the duplicity characteristic of the sinner *in Spiritum sanctum* is likely to appear in a discrepancy between words and deeds[45]—a concept which elsewhere forms part of his definition of a lie.[46] This characteristic obviously applies to the Pardoner, who stirs his hearers to devotion in order to increase his sales. In the bragging confession of his misdeeds there is not a sign of contrition. The same distinction, highly conventional, also forms part of the traditional exegesis of the *lignum aridum* with which Isaiah compared the eunuch. Of the sterile tree St. Augustine remarks in another place, "Folia sola habebat, fructum non habebat . . . : sic sunt qui verba habent, et facta non habent" [47] [Leaves alone it had, it had no fruit . . . : even so are those who have words but have not deeds].

[45] See *Epist. ad Romanos, inchoata expositio (PL*, xxxv, col. 2105–2106): "Verbum enim dicere, non ita videtur hic positum, ut tantummodo illud intelligatur quod per linguam fabricamus, sed quod corde conceptum, etiam opere exprimimus. Sicut enim non confitentum Deum, qui tantum oris sono confitentur, non etiam bonis operibus. . . . Sic etiam qui hoc verbum, quod sine venia vult intelligi Dominus, in Spiritum sanctum dicit, hoc est, qui desperans de gratia et pace quam donat, in peccatis suis perseverandum sibi esse dicit, dicere intelligendus est factis, ut quomodo illi factis Dominum negant, sic isti factis dicant se in mala vita sua et perditis moribus perseveraturos, et ita faciant, hoc est perseverent." [For 'to speak a word' does not seem here to be meant in this way, to be understood as only that which we form with the tongue, but also as that which we have conceived in our hearts, and which we express by our works; even as those do not acknowledge God who do so only with the sound of their voices and not with good works. . . . Thus whoever speaks so against the Holy Spirit, speaks that word that the Lord will take without favor—that is, whoever, despairing of the grace and peace which He gives, says that he must continue in his sins—is to be understood as speaking with actions, so that, even as some deny the Lord by their actions, so these say by their actions that they will persevere in their evil life and corrupt practices, and they do so—that is, persevere.] The reference to the false confession should be noted.

[46] Some idea of the pervasive significance of duplicity may be gained from Augustine's tractate, *de mendacio*. See also Col. iii 9; Eph. iv 25; and n. 29, above. The Parson is, again, just the opposite: "first he wroghte, and afterward he taughte."

[47] *Enarratio in Psalmum CXXVIII*[:6] (*PL*, xxxvii, col. 1688). Compare *PL*, xxxvi, col. 334. So with the Pardoner's "preaching," in contrast to the Parson's, only part of the office is fulfilled—the "letter" rather than the "spirit." *A Late Medieval Tractate on Preaching* states: "Jesus undertook to do and to teach, or rather, first to do and then to teach. To denote this, each faithful preacher today is held to preaching first by deed and then by sermon. Would indeed that each preacher were to become such a diligent imitator of Jesus Christ, that he should preach not with the word alone but also with works!" [trans. Harry Caplan, in *Studies in Rhetoric*

III

I have tried thus far to indicate that the three terms suggested for identifying the character of the Pardoner—that is, consideration of the man as the conventional *eunuchus non Dei,* as the vetus homo, and as the sinner *in Spiritum sanctum*—are merely different emphases with respect to the same spiritual phenomenon. The eunuch is the *vetus homo,* who by wilfully cutting himself off from grace presumptuously sins against the Holy Spirit. Chaucer suggests this spiritual state by using the image of eunuchry, reinforcing his point by allusions to the concept of the *veteres homines* who, according to Paul, "semetipsos tradiderunt impudicitiae, in operationem immunditiae omnis in avaritiam" [have given themselves to lasciviousness, to working all uncleanness, to avarice] (Eph. iv, 19).

The significance of the concept of the *vetus homo* for an understanding of the character of the Pardoner can be grasped only by examination of all of Paul's statements in their full Scriptural and exegetical context. However, a few details may be mentioned with regard to the statement in Ephesians, iv, 17 ff. A specific reference to this text indicates its importance. To Paul's exhortation to those who have "put off the Old Man": "qui furabitur, jam non furetur; magis autem laboret, operando manibus suis, quod bonum est, ut habet unde tribuat necessitatem patienti" [who would steal, let him steal no longer, but rather labor, working with his hands, which is good, so that he may have what is necessary to give to the sufferer] (iv, 28), the Pardoner retorts, "I wol nat do no labour with myne handes," and engages rather in thievery of spiritual offerings.[48] Through his false preaching he also identifies himself with the *vetus homo.* "Propter quod deponentes mendacium, loquimini veritatem unusquisque cum proximo suo" [Wherefore, putting aside lying, let each one of you speak the truth with his neighbor] (iv, 25) is further developed in iv, 29: "Omnis sermo malus ex ore vestro non procedat: sed si quis bonus ad aedificationem fidei, ut det gratiam audientibus" [Let no evil speech come forth from your mouth; but whatever sort is good for the building up of faith, so that it might give grace to its hearers]. In this activity, we have seen, the Pardoner should specifically take part. The phraseology here is echoed by that of Rupertus concerning the

---

and Public Speaking in Honor of James A. Winans (New York, 1926), p. 72: cited by C. O. Chapman, "Chaucer on Preachers and Preaching," *PMLA,* XLIV (1929), 184].

When considered as a class, it is apparent that the *steriles* or *aridi ligni* are the same as the *arbor malorum* which the Pardoner takes as "his theme." In a sense, his tale may thus be quite literally about himself. See below, n. 60.

[48] Not recorded in Robinson's notes. Fansler, *op. cit.,* p. 164, says Chaucer imitates Faux-Semblant's statement, "Sans james de mains traveiller" (*RR* 12504), which follows the same text.

eunuch. Neither the Old Man nor the eunuch, it may be added, abides by the precept which follows immediately: "Et nolite constristare Spiritum sanctum" [And do not grieve the Holy Spirit] (iv, 30).

In portraying the Pardoner of Rouncevale, then, Chaucer provides the *cortex* of his description with details which individualize his character, but which also expose for the reader a *nucleus* of deeper significance. By recalling the conventional concepts of the false eunuch and of the *vetus homo,* they help to identify the nature and enormity of the Pardoner's sin. He emerges as a type of the false ecclesiastic—the eunuch "qui specie religionis simulat castitatem" [who counterfeits chastity with the appearance of religion]. Among the pilgrims of the *Canterbury Tales* he stands at the opposite pole from the Parson, the true leader in the Church, who strives

> To shewe you the wey, in this viage,
> Of thilke parfit glorious pilgrymage
> That highte Jerusalem celestial:
>
> (X.49–51)

that is, the straight and narrow "wey" [49] which Christ identifies with Himself. On the other hand, the Pardoner, dealing as he does with spiritual merchandise, commits the most vicious and dangerous hypocrisy possible. Of the characters on the pilgrimage to Canterbury he is the representative of the false leader within the Church, who "commissum habens talentum verbi Dei, multorum bene possit operari et utiliter negotiari, vacat otio, et acceptam indigne gratiam negligit" [though having the responsibility of the word of God entrusted to him, whereby he might be capable of good works and fruitful tasks for the edification of many, has time for idleness and meanly ignores available grace]. He will not make baskets nor counterfeit the apostles. Cloaked in the outward aspects of his office, he wilfully misdirects those whom he can move. As he says, he "saffrons" his speech with Latin

> . . . for to stire hem to devocioun.
> Thanne shewe I forth my longe cristal stones . . .
>
> (346–47)

The shift in intent expressed between these two lines dramatizes his tactics, the gap between his *verba* and *facta*—his "handes" and his "tonge." It parallels significantly his concluding effort with Harry Bailly. The relics in those "stones" turn the love of his victim from God and into *amor sui,* reversing the proper ladder of love, for they claim to provide increase in temporal or earthly treasure. As a selling technique he makes his hearers "soore to repente."

---

[40] Matth. vii, 14; Heb. xii, 14; etc.

The "wey," therefore, that the Pardoner shows "in this viage" is the opposite to that pointed out by the Parson. The Parson's way is through penitence;[50] the Pardoner's, although he knows the better path, through impenitence in evil. Sterile in good works, wilfully sinning against the Holy Ghost, he remains boastfully impenitent in full knowledge of his sin. Chaucer has produced a daring and effective irony in creating as his Pardoner the eunuch who presumptuously glories in the one unpardonable sin.

IV

Rupertus' method in analyzing the concept of the eunuch may be applied to a great variety of signs, with much the same results. A case in point is Professor Robertson's illustration of the mediaeval treatment of gardens, trees, flowers and related symbols. As he says, "similar studies might be made of names, numbers, animals, stones, or other things," [51] and they might be similarly documented. When the more familiar Scriptural images appear literally in the *cortex* of Christian art, they immediately suggest one of their spiritual analogies which are themselves usually twofold, referring to their significance in both Jerusalem and Babylon. We may often determine the exact spiritual analogy only from context, since the opposite spiritual equivalent is usually implied. Concepts such as the concept of Death may be considered literally, as the rioters themselves do in the tale, still preserving the spiritual opposition—in this case, death to sin (Rom. vi, 11) or death to Christ or life (Col. iii, 4).[52] To use pertinent terms, the concepts of either the death of the *vetus homo* or the death of the *novus homo* may be symbolized by physical death. Thus, taking an example from the *Pardoner's Tale,* the literal image of the treasure suggests the spiritual opposites of Matthew, vi, 19. In the context of the tale we recognize that the rioters do not find the "true" treasure (in which the "povre" Parson is "rich") they should have laid up in heaven, but the "false" earthly treasure which is itself the death they seek—as was understood by the hermit of the analogue in the *Cento Antiche Novelle.* The concept of the heavenly treasure, strongly implied, stresses how far down the "croked" way the rioters have gone.

In these terms I wish now to outline briefly an interpretation of the tale itself, in which the calculated description of the Pardoner may be seen to be functionally appropriate. Recognizing the importance of the form of the sermon (one of the effects of which is to throw the Pardoner into bolder contrast with the Parson) and of the theological subdivisions of its *expositio* for a detailed analysis of the *Pardoner's*

[50] Cf. *ParsT.* 75–80.
[51] *Op. cit., Speculum,* XXVI (1951), 25.
[52] Cf. *ParsT.* 183–184.

Tale, I confine my attention here almost exclusively to the *exemplum* intended to illustrate his exposition of the theme: *Radix malorum est Cupiditas.* One of the best conceived stories in all literature, this *exemplum* possesses an undeniable universality, provocative despite any change in systems of values. I feel, however, that an interpretation based on Chaucer's use of Scriptural imagery, without precluding others, provides an additional dimension of philosophical importance.

The Pardoner—this *quaestor*—himself a seeker after the false treasure, tells a tale of seekers after Death. We should remember that the basic concern of the *exemplum* is Death. Death in the tale is the literal result of each of the aspects of *cupiditas* distinguished in the *expositio.* The tale is first an example showing the evils of drunkenness, that "verray sepulture Of mannes wit and his discrecioun." The rioters' day begins in drink, to the solemn background of their "fordronke" [53] comrade's funeral bell, and ends in death, brought to two of the three in a bottle of wine. They swear, furthermore, an oath of brotherhood, the breaking of which leads directly to death. After they find their treasure they draw lots to decide who is to bring back the "breed and wyn," and *hasardrye* becomes involved in all the murders.

Ironically, the Pardoner, of course, is himself a chief offender with regard to most of the vices he treats in his sermon. He will not tell his tale until he has eaten and drunk his fill.

> "It shal be doon," quod he, "by Seint Ronyon!
> But first," quod he, "heere at this alestake
> I wol bothe drynke, and eten of a cake."
>
> (320–22)

He is a man of many oaths (*Ronyan,* in both French and English a word for the "coillons," is an appropriate saint for a eunuch to swear by). More generally, as the *vetus homo* and the *aridum lignum* of spiritual eunuchry, he is the literal embodiment of *cupiditas,* the larger theme of his sermon.

> Therfore *my* theme is yet, and evere was,
> *Radix malorum est Cupiditas.* (425–26)

Death is conceived in the *exemplum* in the variety of senses implicit in Christian thought. Death of either the *vetus homo* or the *novus homo* is the *modus vivendi* of the other: a phenomenon suggested by Chaucer's metaphor of eunuchry, and expressed by the Pardoner himself:

[53] Drunkenness tropologically symbolizes spiritual blindness, love of temporalia: i.e., spiritual death. Cf. Robertson and Huppé, *Piers Plowman, op. cit.,* pp. 40, 52, 110–111.

> But, certes, he that haunteth swiche delices
> Is deed, whil that he lyveth in tho vices.
>
> (547-48)

In attempting to "slay" Death, then, the rioters do not engage in an
entirely meaningless quest. Adam's fall brought death, both physical
and spiritual, into the world, and all men after, born in his image,
have been mortal. The virtuous man *should* slay Death, the inheritance of the Old Man. By crucifixion and burial of this "earthly
image"—the "body of sin"—the soul may put on the image of Christ
and achieve its heavenly treasure in eternal life, the inheritance of
the New Man. As Christ slew Death upon the Cross, so his followers
can gain eternal life and cause the death of Death.

The symbolic quest of the rioters to cause their version of the death
of Death is significantly introduced.

> In Flaundres whilom was a compaignye
> Of yonge folk that haunteden folye,
> As riot, hasard, stywes, and tavernes,
> Where as with harpes, lutes, and gyternes,
> They daunce and pleyen at dees bothe day and nyght,
> And eten also and drynken over hir myght,
> Thurgh which they doon the devel sacrifise
> Withinne that develes temple, in cursed wise,
> By superfluytee abhomynable.   (463-71)

Like the Pardoner himself, they are classed ironically as "yonge folk."
That these men are literally but not spiritually "young" is apparent
from Chaucer's compact exposition. Dancing the "olde daunce,"
subjecting themselves to fortune in their play, engaging in the false
banquet of sense, "they doon the devel sacrifise Withinne that develes
temple."

> And right anon thanne comen tombesteres
> Fetys and smale, and yonge frutesteres,
> Syngeres with harpes, baudes, wafereres,—
>
> (477-79)

the purveyors of the "olde daunce," the false feast, the *vetus canticum*
—"Whiche been the verray develes officeres." Into this atmosphere of
spiritual death is introduced the spectre of physical death: "they herde
a belle clynke Biforn a cors, was caried to his grave."

The irony of the situation is now heightened. One of the rioters
tells his "knave" to ask the corpse's name. The "boy" provides not
only this information, but also some suitable advice.

> "And, maister, er ye come in [Death's] presence,
> Me thynketh that it were necessarie

> For to be war of swich an adversarie.
> Beth redy for to meete hym everemoore;
> Thus taughte me my dame; I say namoore."
> "By seinte Marie!" seyde this taverner,
> "The child seith sooth. . . .   (680–86)
> To been avysed greet wysdom it were,
> Er that he dide a man a dishonour."   (690–91)

The advice of the "child" can be duplicated endlessly in sermons and moral tracts. One should be ready to meet death at all times in view of the judgment after death.[54] The "truth" of the young man's assertion has been recognized, however, by few other than the taverner. As a point of departure for the tale the false "yonge folk" literalize (and thus pervert) the word of the true "young man," [55] whose "dame" is the Church,[56] the source of such doctrine. They set out to seek a literal Death.

Having perverted the counsel of the *novus homo,* the rioters turn for advice to a mysterious "olde man" who directs them on their way. Their search is not fruitless. The Death they discover, however, is no literal "traytour," but *spiritual* death which their spiritual blindness prevents them from recognizing: the gold which turns their hearts from the life of their souls.[57] It is clear that this is the false "treasure" —almost eight bushels of earthly treasure: the opposite of the eternal treasure which should be laid up in heaven. The quest of Death personified and the resultant physical death of the revellers emphasize the real spiritual death found under the oak tree to which the old man guides them. Physical death comes to all; but spiritual death is the root of all evil.

The circumstances in which the treasure is discovered reinforce this identification. Although he says that he seeks Death himself, the old man points the way:

---

[54] Cf., e.g., *ParsT.* 157 ff.

[55] The figure of the "youth" as man spiritually regenerate is as traditional as that of his opposite, the Old Man. Alanus defines "*Juvenis,* proprie dicitur renovatus per gratiam" ['Young' properly means restored through grace] (*Distinctiones, PL,* ccx, col. 825); "*Juventus,* proprie, innovatio virtutum" ['Youth,' properly, a renewal of virtues] (*ibid.*). The *Allegoriae in sacram Scripturam* of Rabanus Maurus (*PL,* cxii, col. 975) defines "*Juventus,* reversio ad bonum, ut in Psalmis: 'Renovabitur ut aquila vita tua [Ps. cii, 5],' id est ad instar aquilae a pravi vetustate" ['Youth,' reversion to the good, as in the Psalm: "Your life will be renewed like the eagle's" (Ps. cii.5), that is, to the likeness of an eagle from crooked old age]. Isidore's *Etymology* includes the following: "*Puer* . . . pro obsequio et fidei puritate" ['Boy' . . . (used) for obedience and purity of faith] (*PL,* LXXXII, col. 416).

[56] Cf. Gal. iv, 26.

[57] This is the treasure for which the Pardoner strives, and that to which he directs the souls of those who buy his "relikes." Cf. Col. iii, 4.

> "Now, sires," quod he, "if that ye be so leef
> To fynde Deeth, turne up this croked wey,
> For in that grove I lafte hym, by my fey,
> Under a tree, and there he wole abyde;
> Noght for youre boost he wole him no thyng hyde."
>
> (760–64)

Death, he says, lies up the "croked wey"—the opposite of the straight and narrow; "in that grove"—that is, in the false paradise of cupidity;[58] and "under a tree"—*in medio ligni,* where Adam and Eve lost their true Eden and found Death first.[59] In terms of mediaeval Christian imagery, this is surely the way to find Death, but not the way to slay him. Furthermore, if the *exemplum* as a whole illustrates the Pardoner's theme, in a sense the oak tree under which the gold is discovered literally exemplifies the words of his text, *Radix malorum est Cupiditas.* For this tree may itself be regarded as the *arbor malorum* —the tree of evil (or of death)[60]—whose root is cupidity symbolized by the golden earthly treasure. This tree, whose *radix* is cupiditas, is also a version of the symbolic sterile tree to which the eunuch is compared by Isaiah.

It is finally appropriate that the director on the "croked wey" should be the old man, who thus assumes a position in the tale suggestively analogous to that of the teller.[61] Spiritual death is arrived at by failing to follow the counsel of the *novus homo* in preference to that of the *vetus homo.* The cupidinous desires of the fallen aspect of man not only point out the way of perdition, the false paradise and the tree of death, but in a sense create them. In the tale the figure of the old man stands as a symbolic opposite to that of the tavern boy.

Like the youth, the old man refers to his mother:

> Thus walke I, lyk a restelees kaityf,
> And on the ground, which is my moodres gate,
> I knokke with my staf, bothe erly and late,
> And seye "Leeve mooder, leet me in!"
>
> (728–31)

In contrast to the youth, he is of the generation of the earth, earthy. There is a broad suggestion of the "earthly image" of Adam, the *vetus homo,* the antithesis of the *imago Christi,* or *novus homo.*[62] Like the

[58] See Robertson, *op. cit., Speculum,* XXVI (1951), *passim.*

[59] *Ibid.,* esp. pp. 25–26.

[60] The Parson describes the *lignum vitae,* its opposite, in some detail: cf. *ParsT.* 112–126. Cf. Robertson, *op. cit., Speculum,* XXVI (1951), 25–27.

[61] The old man has been variously identified: as the personification of Death; as the personification of Old Age; as the Wandering Jew—that remnant of the Old Law who wanders through Christendom seeking to die; and most recently as just an aged man. Identification as the *vetus homo* has not previously been made.

[62] Cf. I. Cor. xv, 45–49, esp. 48–49; John iii, 31; etc.

wandering Jew, the Old Man of whom Paul wrote cannot die, and will not die so long as human nature does not change. Significantly the revellers refer to him as a spy of Death, an ally of Death, and he is dressed in a shroud—"al forwrapped" save his face: for the *vetus homo* represents the state of spiritual death. He desires "an heyre clowt to wrappe" himself in—i.e. the hair shirt of penance, and he wishes to be buried: for the Old Man must be crucified and buried that the New Man may live. The *vetus homo* may die only by the assumption of the *novus homo*. This familiar concept lies behind a significant passage which previous discussions of the old man have avoided: his response to the question of the rioters:

> "Why lyvestow so longe in so greet age?"
> This olde man gan looke in his visage,
> And seyde thus, "For I ne kan nat fynde
> A man, though that I walked into Ynde,
> Neither in citee ne in no village,
> *That wolde chaunge his youthe for myn age;*
> And therefore moot I han myn age stille,
> As longe tyme as it is Goddes wille."
>
> (719–26)

Like the Pardoner, this old man can quote Scripture to his own purpose;[63] his mouth is full of verbal holiness. Like the Pardoner, too, in full knowledge he points the way to spiritual death, directing the "riotoures" up the "croked wey" into the garden of cupidity, just as the desires of the *vetus homo* lead any soul astray. Lacking that peace which passeth understanding, he wanders a "restelees kaityf," in a manner reminiscent of a description provided by the Parson with respect to the Judgment of the *veteres homines:*

> Right so fareth the peyne of helle; it is lyk deeth for the horrible angwissh, and why? For it peyneth hem evere, as though they sholde dye anon; but certes, they shal nat dye. / For, as seith Seint Gregorie, "To wrecche caytyves shal be deeth withoute deeth, and ende withouten ende, and defaute withoute failynge. / For hir deeth shal alwey lyven, and hir ende shal everemo bigynne, and hir defaute shal nat faille." / And therfore seith Seint John the Evaungelist: "They shullen folwe deeth, and they shul nat fynde hym; and they shul desiren to dye, and deeth shal flee fro hem." [64]

[63] He quotes the Old Law: Leviticus, xix, 32, according to the letter. Cp., e.g., the comment of Rabanus Maurus (*PL*, cviii, col. 460) on this verse: "Canum autem vere senem, id est, eum qui sapientia profectus est, intelliget." [He (Moses) understands the hoary-headed to be truly the old man, that is, one who is advanced in wisdom.] Rabanus' gloss reflects an opposite sense of figurative age than that understood with reference to the *vetus homo.*

[64] *ParsT*. 213–216. The Scriptural citation is to Apoc. ix, 6. "Kaityf" etymologically derives from *captivus* (i.e., in context, thrall to sin).

The result of the old man's direction is death, both spiritual and physical. The old bottles for which the "yongeste" reveller runs are filled not with the new wine of grace, but with the poison of the Old Law;[65] and the *exemplum* closes with a picture of the false feast at which such wine is drunk.

> "Now lat us sitte and drynke, and make us merie,
> And afterward we wol his body berie."
>
> (883–84)

This *convivium* under the oak, with its reversed sacramental "breed and wyn," serves to symbolize the subjection of these Cain-like "brothers" to their earthly treasure; and recalls the Pardoner's own repast at the "ale-stake." The *exemplum* pictures the discovery and the effect of the "root of all evil."

V

The extraordinarily tight-knit organization of the *Pardoner's Tale* does not permit full explication in a limited space. Other details of the *cortex* might be shown to be similarly significant. What should be clear, however, is the consistent philosophical pattern artistically presented through the manipulation of Scriptural images, the main points of which have here been suggested rather than defined. The import of the *nucleus* is thus a consistent exemplification of the Pardoner's text.

It should also be more evident how the *Pardoner's Tale* fits generally into a scheme of opposition between Charity and Cupidity in the *Canterbury Tales* as a whole. The extreme maliciousness of the Pardoner as a person sets him at the far end of the scale among the pilgrims. As a type he is even more definitely evil. He is the false eunuch who stands and points the way up the wrong road. He represents the way of cupidity, malice, impenitence, spiritual sterility—just the opposite of the way of the Parson and his spiritual brother, the Plowman.[66]

[65] Matth. ix, 17: *Neque mittit vinum novum in utres veteres.* [Neither does a man put new wine in old bottles.] *The Glossa Ordinaria* refers to Jerome, who says, "Veteres utres debemus intelligere Scribas et Pharisaeos" [by old bottles we ought to understand the Scribes and Pharisees] which hold the Old Law (*Commentar. in Evangelium Matthaei* [*PL*, XXVI, col. 59]). Only the "old wine" of *carnalitas* will fill the *utres veteres:* cf. St Augustine, *Sermo CCLXVII* (*PL*, XXXVIII, col. 1230). Bede, *In Matthaei Evangelium Expositio* (*PL*, XCII, col. 48), glosses: "Utres veteres fuerunt apostoli ante infusionem Spiritus sancti. . . . Vino . . . novo fervor fidei, spei et charitatis, exprimitur, quo in novitatem sensus nostri reformamur." [The old bottles were the apostles before the infusion of the Holy Spirit . . . in new wine is expressed the ardor of faith, hope and charity, by which we are remade anew in our understanding.] The "new wine" of grace causes spiritual *ebrietas:* cp. n. 53.

[66] Cf. the Parson's text and his "glose" of it: *ParsT.* 75 ff. For the symbolic Plowman cf. Robertson and Huppé. *Piers Plowman, op. cit.,* pp. 17–19.

He is that Old Man as he lives and exerts his influence in the great pilgrimage of life. And as the *vetus homo* he is to be opposed to the Christlike figure of the *novus homo,* the true guide—the "povre PER-SOUN OF A TOUN."

Unfortunately, as Chaucer pictures his world, both exist *in ecclesia.* Utilizing the various levels of meaning connected with the idea of the Church,[67] we can see more clearly the full significance of the Pardoner in Chaucer's total conception. If we consider the literal Church, this Pardoner may be thought of as representing the evil ecclesiastic—the unregenerate hypocrite who undermines its structure from within: the wolf in sheep's clothing. If the Church is thought of as the whole congregation of the faithful—that is, as Christian society—the Pardoner is representative of those insidious, malicious evils that bring *confusio* into society. If the idea of the Church is looked at tropologically—from the point of view of human nature—that is, as the soul of the individual, this Pardoner is a representation of that Old Man of whom Paul wrote. Anagogically, the *vetus homo* is the devil himself, from whose "temple" the rioters begin their quest. The analogy may be carried out on all of these levels. In each case this Old Man must be crucified and buried before confusion and Death may be conquered. For each level of allegory the figure represents the appropriate *radix malorum.*

Behind Chaucer's conception of the Pardoner and his tale lies the familiar Christian thesis that all men should be *quaestores*—not, like the Pardoner, for the material treasure, but for what the Pardoner should seek, the spiritual "offertorie." They should seek not the false pardons of which the Pardoner's wallet is so "bret-ful," but that pardon which Chaucer cannot forbear mentioning albeit in the words of the Pardoner: that is, the Pardon of "Jesu Crist, that is oure soules leche." Important also is the concept that all should be seekers of Death, too—but the death of that Old Man, through whose burial Death is really conquered; and who must be put down before we cease to find *confusio,* or disorder, such as that which literally breaks out between the Pardoner and Harry Bailly at the end of this tale. And it is clear that this is a spiritual matter. All the worthy Knight can do as representative of the temporal arm of the law is to make a temporary peace—an earthly equivalent of the *visio pacis.* But the Old Man still goes on wandering through the world, glaring with sterile lust out of his hare-like eyes.

[67] Cf., e.g., Hugh of St Victor, *Sermons* I–III (*PL,* CLXXVII, cols. 901–907), where the idea of the Church receives detailed treatment according to the conventional levels of allegory. The *vetus homo* transforms *Ecclesia* into "that develes temple."

Old Age and *Contemptus Mundi* in *The Pardoner's Tale*

by *John M. Steadman*

In the old man of *The Pardoner's Tale,* scholars have detected an embarrassing profusion of meanings. Bushnell stressed his affinities with the Wandering Jew. In Robinson's opinion, he was "a symbol of Death itself, or possibly of Old Age, conceived as Death's messenger." Mrs. Hamilton argued that "if Chaucer's character was meant to be anything more than a pathetic old man who has outlived all zest for living, he must stand for Old Age as the Harbinger of Death. . . ." Miss Strang has maintained that, since "the Old Man's speech . . . introduces a great deal of information to which no literal meaning can be assigned," it ought, accordingly, to be interpreted allegorically. On the other hand, Owen rejected the allegorical approach entirely. Chaucer was simply describing a "notion of aged humanity" he "could have found already well developed" in Maximianus, and "the old man is merely an old man." [1]

We are confronted, then, by two related, but unresolved problems—(1) whether Chaucer's old man should be interpreted allegorically, and (2) if so, which of several alternative interpretations is the most pertinent and the most probable.

"Old Age and Contemptus Mundi *in* The Pardoner's Tale*" by John M. Steadman. From* Medium Ævum, *XXXIII (1964), 121–30. Translations have been supplied by the editor. Published for the Society for the Study of Mediæval Languages and Literature by Basil Blackwell. Reprinted by permission of the publisher.*

[1] N. S. Bushnell "The Wandering Jew and *The Pardoner's Tale,*" *SP* XXVIII (1931) 450–460; F. N. Robinson (ed.) *The Complete Works of Geoffrey Chaucer* (London 1957) p. 731; Marie Padgett Hamilton "Death and Old Age in *The Pardoner's Tale,*" *SP* XXXVI (1939) 571–576; W. J. B. Owen "The Old Man in *The Pardoner's Tale,*" *RES, NS* II (1951) 49–55; G. C. Sedgewick "The Progress of Chaucer's Pardoner, 1880–1940," *MLQ* I (1940), 431–458; Barbara M. H. Strang, "Who is the Old Man in 'The Pardoner's Tale'?" *N&Q, NS* VII (1960) 207–208. The essays by Owen and Sedgewick are reprinted in *Chaucer: Modern Essays in Criticism,* ed. Wagenknecht (New York 1959) pp. 126–165. Also relevant are articles by P. Miller *Speculum* XXX (1955) 180–199, G. R. Coffman *Speculum* IX (1934) 249–277 and A. L. Kellogg *Speculum* XXXVI (1951) 479.

I

Before attempting to answer either of these questions directly, let us examine some of the arguments on which these various interpretations have been based. A chain is only as strong as its weakest link, and there appear to be several flaws in the current arguments for and against allegorical interpretation.

1. In Owen's opinion, it was "contrary to the logic of allegory that Old Age as the messenger of Death should appear to a company of young men." Though this may indeed seem to violate logic, it *does*, nevertheless, occur in allegory. *Piers Plowman,* in fact, provides striking evidence against Owen's assumption. In Passus XI, Elde admonishes the dreamer while he is still "ȝonge and ȝepe," with "ȝeres ynowe, Forto lyve longe and ladyes to lovye":

> Thanne was þere one þat hiȝte elde þat hevy was of chere,
> "Man," quod he, "if I mete with þe, bi Marie of hevene,
> Þow shalt fynde fortune þe faille at þi moste nede,
> And *concupiscencia-carnis* clene þe forsake.
> Bitterliche shaltow banne þanne bothe dayes and niȝtes
> Coveytise-of-eyghe þat ever þow hir knewe,
> And pryde-of-parfyt-lyvynge to moche peril þe brynge."
>
> (B XI 26–32)

Like the three rioters, however, the dreamer disregards this warning and plunges into a life of dissipation, while Old Age and Holiness lament his lapse:

> "Allas, eye!" quod elde and holynesse bothe,   ·
> "That witte shal torne to wrecchedness for wille to have his lykynge!"   (43–44)

In the final passus Elde returns, fights with Life, and afflicts the dreamer. Oppressed by old age, the latter—much like Chaucer's old man—beseeches Nature ("kynde") for release (XX 200).

2. In view of the marked affinities between Chaucer's old man and the *senex* of Maximianus' First Elegy, it seems difficult to accept Miss Strang's argument that no ordinary old man is "rejected by Death (C 727); nor is the ground the gate of any ordinary man's mother (C 729), at which he knocks, invoking his mother within (C 737–38)." Maximianus had, in fact, employed these very details in his characteristic portrait of the miseries of old age.[2] Though his manner of expression is obviously figurative and dramatic, the details themselves are

---

[2] G. L. Kittredge "Chaucer and Maximianus," *AJP* IX (1888) 84–85. Cf. also Boethius (pp. 320–321 of Chaucer's translation, ed. Robinson, *op. cit.*).

clearly intended to be typical of the "ordinary old man." Like Chaucer's old man, Maximianus' *senex* is more eloquent than the average old man, but the content of his lament is the common fate of all old men, the *miseria senectutis*.

3. The analogy with Maximianus does not, however, provide absolutely firm support for Owen's conclusion that Chaucer's old man is merely "an old man and nothing more." In the very passage which apparently inspired Chaucer's picture of the aged man knocking at the ground for admittance, Maximianus chose the feminine abstract noun *senectus* (sometimes capitalized, as though it were a personification, like Virgil's *tristis Senectus, Aen.* VI 275), instead of *senex* or the masculine adjective *senectus*:

> Nec cælum spectare licet, sed prona senectus
>   Terram, qua genita est et reditura, videt . . .

> Hinc est quod bacula incumbens ruitura senectus
>   Assiduo pigram verbere pulsat humum . . .[3]

> [He may not look at the heavens, no, stooped Old Age
>   gazes at the earth, whence he arose and to which he will return . . .

> Thus it is that nearly falling Old Age, leaning on a staff,
>   continually strikes the unyielding ground with a blow . . .]

Is Chaucer's old man a personification of old age, or is he merely a typical example of "aged humanity"? Though the analogy with Maximianus' elegy lends a measure of support to either view, it gives stronger probability to the latter interpretation. In the passages quoted above *senectus* can mean either "old age" or "old men." [4] Elsewhere in the elegy Maximianus tends to use the terms *senex* and *senectus* virtually interchangeably. The speaker—the *persona*—in the Latin poem is, moreover, not Old Age, but an old man, lamenting the miseries of old age. This is obvious from the first lines of the elegy, where the aged speaker (the *senex*) apostrophizes Old Age (*senectus*):

> Æmula quid cessas finem properare senectus?
>   Cur et in hoc fesso corpore tarda venis?
> Solve precor miseram tali de carcere vitam:
>   Mors est iam requies, vivere poena mihi.
> Non sum qui fueram: periit pars maxima nostri;
>   Hoc quoque quod superest languor et horror habent.[5]

---

[3] *Poetae Latini Minores* ed. Aemilius Baehrens (Leipzig 1883) p. 326; cf. p. 328, "incurva senectus."

[4] Nisard, in fact, renders *prona senectus* as *vieillard,* but *ruitura senectus* as *vieillesse* (p. 594).

[5] Baehrens, p. 317.

[Old Age, vying with me, why do you stop hastening the end?
Why are you coming so slowly in this tired body?
Please release my wretched life from this imprisonment:
At this point death is repose, living a punishment for me.
I am not who I was: the greatest part of me is gone;
Weariness and dread hold what is left.]

The speaker here is clearly the typical *senex*, describing the characteristic *incommoda senectutis*. The same may be said of Chaucer's figure.

Though the aged stranger of *The Pardoner's Tale* is not Old Age, he is not simply "an old man and nothing more." Owen has failed to distinguish between "an old man" and a "notion of aged humanity." The very details Chaucer apparently borrowed from Maximianus indicate his concern for the general idea rather than the individual example, for the universal rather than the particular. The aged man whom the rioters encounter is important primarily as a type rather than as an individual. He is the *senex* par excellence—not merely *an* old man, but *the* old man. In conveying this abstract concept of the miseries of senility through a concrete example, Chaucer has presented the *universale in re* [the universal in the concrete thing]. His attempt to delineate the general through the particular brings him close to the frontiers of allegory, but he does not actually cross.

4. The old man's relation to the Messenger-of-Death motif also requires re-examination. Does the text really offer us sufficient foundation for the view that he is harbinger of Death? To be sure, Sackville combines the Messenger-of-Death motif with details reminiscent of Maximianus' *senex*. But he also gives us an explicit personification of Old Age[6]—which Chaucer does not do. It is significant that, despite the highly figurative language Chaucer employs in this scene, he makes no overt use of the Messenger-of-Death metaphor. The Pardoner does indeed introduce into his sermon representative instances of sickness, disaster, and old age—the lethal triad of the Messenger poems—but he does not represent them figuratively in terms of the messenger-symbol. Neither sickness nor disaster is personified. Though the tale includes examples of death by pestilence and *aventure*, none of the characters die of old age. Nor is the old man's role that of a messenger. He does indeed inform the rioters where they may find Death, but this is not the office of a messenger, but rather the function of a guide. Though the "other hasardour" accuses the ancient stranger of being Death's "aspye" and "oon of his assent, To sleen us yonge folk," a spy and a messenger are by no means identical, and in fact all three rioters perish by *aventure*, not by old age. If Chaucer had really intended to represent this character as a *nuntius mortis*, he would surely have made a more clear-cut and emphatic use of the Messenger-of-Death symbolism.

[6] See Hamilton, p. 576.

In rejecting this interpretation, however, we are not forced to accept the alternative Mrs. Hamilton has offered us—that the aged stranger must be nothing "more than a pathetic old man who has outlived all zest for living." He is, on the contrary, not simply an individual old man, but a *type*—a representative portrait of the ideal *senex* and the miseries of old age. In the last stage of human life (*senium*) as it approaches death (*ad mortis terminum pervenit*),[7] his predicament is essentially that of the dreamer in the final passage of *Piers Plowman*. Oppressed by old age, both long for death as a release. Chaucer's old man is not "Death's messenger," but he is still a *memento mori*.

II

To concur with Owen's preference for a literal, rather than an allegorical, interpretation of Chaucer's old man, is to be faced with another problem. Why does Chaucer deliberately stress the "greet age" of the old man? The poet's emphasis on the character of the *senex* represents a distinct variation on traditional versions of the treasure-story, and the old man's search for death "is a feature not paralleled in any known analogues of the tale."[8] What is the literary function of this innovation? What bearing does it have on the tale as a whole and on the Pardoner's central theme of avarice?

One of the most obvious features of Chaucer's characterization of the old man is his ethical contrast with the three rioters. The encounter between them juxtaposes youth and age, pride and humility, impatience and patience, blasphemy and piety, "vileinye" and "curteisye," folly and wisdom, avarice and *contemptus mundi*. Though these moral opposites seem self-evident, it seems advisable to discuss them in detail, especially as the old man has been interpreted so frequently in a pejorative or sinister light.

1. The opening lines of the tale call attention to the youth of the rioters ("a companye of yonge folk"). The opposition between youth and age is given explicit expression by the old man (who can find no one willing to "chaunge his youthe for myn age") and also by "this other hasardour" (who regards the stranger as one of Death's "assent, To sleen us yonge folk"). The antithesis of youth and age is also apparent in Maximianus' First Elegy, *Horrent me pueri, nequeo velut ante videri*[9] [Boys shudder at me, I cannot appear as I was before].

The concept of old age receives even stronger emphasis in *The Pardoner's Tale* than the idea of youth. Mrs. Hamilton observed that the term "old man" is applied to [the aged stranger] seven times, "old

---

[7] Cf. *PL* CCIX 262; LXXXIII 81–82.

[8] Frederick Tupper "The Pardoner's Tale" in *Sources and Analogues of Chaucer's Canterbury Tales* ed. W. F. Bryan and Germaine Dempster (Chicago 1941) p. 436.

[9] Baehrens, p. 326.

churl" once, and "age" meaning old age four times. The first remarks
the rioters address to him concern his "greet age," and the concept
acquires further emphasis through his own elegiac complaint concerning the miseries of *senectus* and through his quotation from Leviticus
XIX. 32. Moreover, his warning ("Ne dooth un-to an old man noon harm
now, Na-more than ye wolde men dide to yow In age, if that ye so longe
abyde") bears a striking resemblance to the admonition in Innocent
III's chapter *De incommodis senectutis*:

> Porro nec senes contra juvenem glorientur, nec insolescant juvenes
> contra senem, quia quod sumus iste fuit, erimus quandoque quod hic
> est.[10]

> [Moreover, let not old men be boastful before a youth, nor the young
> haughty to an old man; because what we are he once was, and we will
> sometime be what he is now.]

The implications of the old man's rebuke are obvious. Old age is part
of the inevitable misery of man's lot—*la condition humaine*—and the
same fate awaits the young revellers if they live long enough. Like all
other young men, they are unwilling to "chaunge [their] youthe for
. . . age," but they must.

2. The contrast between youth and age underlies the significant difference between the old man and the rioters in their attitudes toward
death. The *senex* desires death because he suffers from the infirmities
of old age. The *juvenes* attempt to overcome death because they are
young and wish to perpetuate their life of riotous pleasures. For one,
death is a release; for the others, a deadly enemy. We should recall the
similar antithesis expressed in Ecclesiasticus xli. 1–4,

> O mors, quam amara est memoria tua homini pacem habenti in sub-
> stantiis suis . . . et adhuc valenti accipere cibum! O mors, bonum est
> judicium tuum homini indigenti, et qui minoratur viribus, Defecto
> ætate, et cui de omnibus cura est . . . !

> [O death, how bitter is the recollection of you to the man at peace
> among his possessions . . . and him still strong enough to take food!
> O death, good is your judgment to the poor man, and to him who is
> of diminished strength or worn-out age, or to whom everything is trou-
> blesome . . . !]

3. The antithesis between youth and age also has a significant bearing on the theme of repentance. The encounter with the old man should
have induced the rioters to "remember [their] Creator in the days of
[their] youth," but they fail to heed the implicit warning in the spec-
tacle of the *tempus afflictionis*. Characteristically they had already

---

[10] *PL* CCXVII 706. For other parallels with Innocent's *De Contemptu Mundi* in
The Canterbury Tales, see Robinson, pp. 694–696, 729–730. Robinson also notes (p.
731) a resemblance between this passage and Ecclesiasticus viii. 6.

grossly misconstrued two previous exhortations to repent in time (ll.
680–691). In their failure to perceive that "adolescentia . . . et volup-
tas vana sint" [youth . . . and pleasure are empty], they are like the
juvenis of Ecclesiastes xi. 9–xii. 1–7 *(Lætare ergo, juvenis, etc.)*.

4. The very lines which stress the youth of the rioters also declare
that they "haunteden folye, As ryot, hasard, stewes, and tavernes." Their
subsequent behaviour is in keeping with this characterization. They
flagrantly misinterpret the advice to prepare for death ("Beth redy for
to mete him evermore" and "To been avysed greet wisdom it were"),
and rashly assay the impossible—to "sleen this false traytour Death."
Their very words after finding the treasure ("Now let us sitte and
drinke, and make us merie") are patently reminiscent of the remarks of
the rich *stultus* [fool] in Luke xii. 19, *requiesce, comede, bibe, epulare*
[take your ease, eat, drink, and be merry]. In their sensual folly they
ignore the fatal results of avarice and forget Death in their enjoyment
of the treasure.

The old man's wisdom stands in clearer relief by contrast with their
folly. He warns them of the approach of old age in words very similar
to those of Pope Innocent III. Like his counterparts in analogues of
this story, he equates the treasure with death and thus displays a moral
insight unsurpassed by any other character in the tale. He is, in fact,
the only person in *The Pardoner's Tale* who gives expression—however oblique and figurative—to the central theme, *Radix malorum est
cupiditas*. The fact that he expresses it in a veiled metaphor rather than
through a bald and overt statement does not discredit his insight. It
simply lends greater intensity and power to the ethical truth he is
describing.

Chaucer's old man appears, then, to be an example of that "honorable old age" whose essence is "understanding" and "an unspotted
life" (Wisdom iv. 8–9).[11] Like his counterparts in the analogues, he is a
wise man, and in emphasizing his "greet age" Chaucer is exploiting the
conventional link between wisdom and old age. The quotation from
Leviticus reinforces this interpretation. According to Rabanus and
Strabus, the *senex* represents the *sapiens,* and both Old and New Testa-
ments command that he be honoured for his wisdom:

[11] Cf. Rabanus' commentary on this text *(PL* CIX 686), *Senectus enim venerabilis
est non diuturna, neque numero annorum computata. Cani sunt autem sensus hom-
inum, et aetas senectutis vita immaculata. Ostendit quid in senectute quaerendum
sit, quia non aetas corporis, sed maturitas mentis et morum probitas in ea laudatur.
. . .* [For venerable old age is not the long-lived sort, nor is it summed up by a
numbering of years. For aged are the judgments of men, and the period of old age
is one of immaculate life. This shows what is to be sought in old age, because what
is laudatory in it is not the age of the body but the maturity of the mind and the
uprightness of its habits. . . .] Cf. also *The Knight's Tale* 1590 ("In elde is bothe
wysdom and usage").

"Coram cano capite surge," id est sapientem honora: cani enim sunt sensus hominis. De quibus senioribus, id est sapientibus, Paulus dicit: "Presbyteri duplici honore digni habeantur, maxime qui laborant in verbo et doctrina" (1 *Tim.* v). Et Dominus ad Moysen: "Elige septuaginta viros, quos tu nosti, quod seniores sunt populi" *(Exod.* xxiv).[12]

["Stand up in the presence of a white head," that is, honor the wise man: for aged are the judgments of man. Concerning which elders, or wise men, Paul says: "Let the elders be held worthy of a twofold honor, especially those who labor in the word and doctrine" (I Tim. v). And the Lord said to Moses: "Choose seventy men whom you know, because they are the elders of the people" (Exod. xxiv).]

Coram cano capite consurge, et honora personam senis, et time Dominum Deum tuum. . . . Bonum est quidem et eum, qui jam ad canitiem pervenit, honorare. Habet enim tempus aliquid amplius procul dubio ad prudentiam, sed et honorem quem provectioribus impendimus, nos quoque a minoribus merebimur, atque ex hoc ordo bonus vitam nostram in honestate custodiens nobis profligatur. Canum autem vere senem, id est, eum qui sapientia profectus est, intelliget, de quo ait *seniores tuos, et dicent tibi (Deut.* xxxii). Sed et Paulus: *Presbyteri duplici honore digni habeantur, maxime qui laborant in verbo et doctrina.*[13]

["Stand up in the presence of a white head, and honor the person of the old man, and fear the Lord thy God." . . . Indeed it is a good thing also to honor the man who has clearly reached old age, for he has had rather more time, doubtless, for arriving at wisdom; but also, the honor that we confer on those of more advanced age we deserve as well from our juniors, and thence a good arrangement takes up our life, to our continual advantage. For he (Moses) understands the hoary-headed to be truly the old man, that is, one who is advanced in wisdom, concerning whom he said: "(ask) your elders, and they will tell you" (Deut. : xxxii). And also Paul: "Let the elders be held worthy of a twofold honor, especially those who labor in the word and doctrine."]

In contrasting the old man's wisdom with the rioters' folly, Chaucer is closer to the literary tradition behind *The Pardoner's Tale* than recent scholarship has recognized. In the analogues, the old man's counterparts are usually wise and holy men—Christ and his disciples, St. Anthony, holy hermits, a moral philosopher.[14] To credit the pejorative interpretations scholars have frequently attached to Chaucer's figure, one must assume a radical departure from the conventional conception of his character. But this assumption is neither necessary nor probable. The chief differences between the old man and these literary counterparts lie in the emphasis on his old age and his desire for death,

---

[12] *PL* CXIV 832.
[13] *PL* CVIII 460. Miller observes that "Rabanus' gloss reflects an opposite sense of figurative age than that understood with reference to the *vetus homo.*"
[14] Tupper, pp. 415–438.

and these are by no means incompatible with the character of the
sapiens.

5. As a result of these antithetical attributes—youth and old age,
folly and wisdom—Chaucer's characters exhibit sharply contrasted attitudes towards the treasure. For several reasons Owen's view that
"there is nothing in Chaucer to suggest that the old man has seen the
gold"—that "he does not know . . . what the revellers will find
under the tree"—does not seem altogether probable. In the first place,
it is at variance with the tradition behind the tale. In the analogues the
wise men who discover the treasure shun it because they are aware of
the fatal consequences of avarice; there is nothing in Chaucer's story to
suggest that the old man has not passed it by for similar reasons. Secondly, the stranger could hardly have given such precise directions to
the rioters unless he had actually seen—or heard of—the gold. Owen's
suggestion that these detailed instructions are simply an improvised
ruse devised by "senile cunning" defies all laws of probability, and there
is certainly "nothing in Chaucer to suggest" that they are just an im-
provisation. Surely, the most obvious—indeed, the only feasible—
inference we can draw from ll. 760–765 is that, like the holy men of
the analogues, the old man has discovered the gold and deliberately
shunned it because he knows the causal relation between cupidity and
death. The passage points distinctly to his moral insight rather than to
his ignorance. Thirdly, Owen's assumption that, if the old man *had*
known what the revellers would find under the tree, "he ought, according to his earlier speech, to have remained with the gold, seeking his
death in it" proposes an alternative which would have been flagrantly
out of character. Though the old man wishes to die, he does not attempt
to shorten his life through his own agency. He is, instead, resigned to
"han myn age stille, As longe time as it is goddes wille."

Thus, despite his indigence, the "povre" stranger condemns the riches
which ensnare the youthful rioters. The ethical contrast between them
is deepened by a further antithesis—the opposition between avarice
and *contemptus mundi.* According to a *Precatio* formerly attributed to
St. Ambrose, these are logical contraries; and the author concludes a
denunciation of avarice with the prayer,

> . . . semper illius sententiae meminerim, qua dicitur: *Nudus egressus*
> *sum de utero matris meae, nudus revertar illuc* (*Job* 1, 21). Atque illius:
> *Nihil intulimus in hunc mundum, sed nec auferre quid possumus* (1
> *Tim.* vi, 7). Quae nimirum dum pie considerantur, mundi contemptum
> auferre videntur, qui avaritiae contrarius est.[15]
>
> [. . . always I bear in mind that thought which runs: "Naked I came
> out of my mother's womb, and naked shall I return to it" (Job : i, 21).
> Also this: "We brought nothing into this world, neither can we carry

anything away" (I Tim. vi, 7). These things, so long as they are considered piously, seem to gain for one a scorn for worldly things that is the opposite of avarice.]

Significantly, Innocent makes use of the same concepts as an argument against avarice; in his *De Contemptu Mundi sive de Miseria Conditionis Humanæ,* he declares that

> Omnis cupidus et avarus contra naturam nititur et molitur. Natura enim pauperem adducit in mundum, natura pauperem reducit a mundo: nudum namque eum terra suscepit, nudum etiam suscipiet: cupidus autem cupit et curat fieri dives in mundo.[16]

> [Every covetous and avaricious person struggles and sets himself against nature. For nature leads a man into the world a pauper and leads him out of it again a pauper: for naked the earth raised him up and naked also will she receive him. Yet the covetous man persists in his desires, and his care is to become rich in the world.]

Old and poor, Chaucer's *senex* is representative of the misery of man's condition. In his readiness to return to the earth his mother, stripped of all possessions except a "heyre clout," [17] he demonstrates

---

[16] *PL* CCXVII 723.

[17] In Robinson's opinion (p. 731), the "cheste" the old man is willing to exchange for a hair-cloth is not a coffin, but a "clothes-chest." It may, of course, contain other worldly goods, including whatever money he may possess. His willingness to part with this "cheste" is a further instance of *contemptus mundi,* analogous to his indifference to the treasure.

If (as several editors think) the "cheste" is a "box containing his property," and the "heyre clout" a "haircloth for burial," then the old man appears to be voicing a commonplace of both classical and Biblical tradition, and highly appropriate to the theme of the Pardoner's sermon. The contrast between man's worldly possessions and the native nakedness with which he enters and leaves the world had long been a conventional argument against love of riches. Cf. Boethius ed. cit. (pp. 330–331); the two texts quoted by St. Ambrose (see fn. 15, *supra*); and Eccl. v. 14. These three texts are closely associated in patristic exegesis as admonitions against avarice, and in several respects they have affinities with the content and imagery of the old man's speech. Like Chaucer's *senex,* Job i. 21 and Ecclesiastes v. 14 refer to the earth metaphorically as the "mother" to whom man must return stripped of his worldly possessions (*nudus*). Though 1 Timothy vi. 7 makes the same point without metaphor, its immediate context is, significantly, the very passage which furnishes the Pardoner with his theme, *Radix malorum est Cupiditas.* As these texts express essentially the same antithesis as the contrast between the old man's "cheste" and "heyre clout," Chaucer may (it seems) have reinforced "the special point" derived from Maximianus—the detail of "the old man knocking on the ground with his staff and calling upon his mother Earth to let him in" (Kittredge, pp. 84–85)—with the point of the Biblical texts which employ the same earth-mother imagery.

Like Maximianus' *senex* (Baehrens V 326), Chaucer's old man beseeches the earth, his *genetrix,* to receive him (*Suscipe me genetrix, nati miserere laborum: [Membra peto gremio fessa fovere tuo . . .]* [Receive me, mother, take pity on the labors of your son: (I beg you to enfold my weary limbs in your bosom . . .)], but the nakedness with which he must return to her—*nudus* except for his shroud—is characteris-

not only his misery, but also his awareness of *la condition humaine*. His poverty itself is emblematic; he can take nothing with him to the grave except his shroud.

Both Maximianus and Job employ the earth-mother metaphor, and Chaucer appears to have combined details reminiscent of both. In their new context they serve not only to express the miseries of old age, but also to convey the antithesis between *contemptus mundi* and *cupiditas*.

6. In contrast to the old man's *contemptus mundi*, the rioters are lovers of the world, *mundi dilectores*. Unlike the stranger, they ignore the true condition of man, and their quest to slay Death is (like avarice itself) *contra naturam*. Where the old man exhibits the truth of 1 John ii. 17, that *mundas transit, et concupiscentia ejus* [the world passes away, and its lusts also], the revellers manifest the three worldly vices —"the lust of the flesh, and the lust of the eyes, and the pride of life." According to Innocent, *Concupiscentia carnis ad voluptates, concupiscentia oculorum ad opes, superbia vitæ pertinet ad honores. Opes generant cupiditates et avaritiam: voluptates pariunt gulam et luxuriam: honores nutriunt superbiam et jactantiam*[18] [The lust of the flesh has to do with physical pleasures, that of the eyes with wealth, and the pride of life with honors. Wealth gives rise to covetousness and avarice; physical pleasures bring forth gluttony and lust; honors foster pride and boasting]. *Concupiscentia carnis* is evident in the rioters' addiction to the delights of the tavern—gluttony, lechery and the like. *Superbia vitæ* is apparent in the insolent behaviour of the "proudest of thise ryotoures" towards the old man. *Concupiscentia oculorum* is manifested in the fascination of the treasure, and it is significant that Chaucer stresses its visual appeal:

> But ech of hem so glad was of that sighte,
> For that the floryns been so faire and brighte . . .
>
> (773–74)

---

tic less of Maximianus' figure than of the universal lot of man as described in Job and Ecclesiastes.

For the interpretation of *utero matris* as a reference to *terra*, see St. Gregory's *Moralia* (*PL* LXXV 570–571); St. Jerome (*PL* XXIII 1057); St. Bruno (*PL* CLXIV 558), etc.

[18] *PL* CCXVII 717. Cf. Bede (*PL* XCIII 93), "*Concupiscentia oculorum est . . . in acquirendis rebus temporalibus*" ["Lust of the eyes" is . . . in acquiring temporal things]; St. Martinus Legionensis (*PL* CCIX 262–263), "*Nolite diligere mundum, id est abundantiam mundi, vel pulchritudinem ejus; neque ea, quae in mundo sunt, ut aurum, argentum, et omnem fluxum divitiarum . . . et concupiscentia oculorum quando visus delectatur, ut in pulchris vestibus, et auro, et talibus . . .*" ["Do not value the world," that is, the abundance of the world or its beauty; nor the things that are in the world, like gold, silver, and its whole flow of riches . . . "and the lust of the eyes" when the sight is delighted, as by beautiful clothes, and gold, and such things . . .].

Ful ofte in herte he rolleth up and doun
The beautee of thise floryns newe and brighte.

(838–39)

The rioters' "hasardrye" is closely related to the Pardoner's theme, for *The Parson's Tale* discusses this vice under the heading of *Avaricia*.

7. There is a further contrast between the old man's meekness and the rioters' pride[19] when they first meet. He greets them "ful mekely" as "lordes" and "sirs" or with blessings ("god you see!" "And god be with yow, wher ye go or ryde," "God save yow, that boghte agayn mankinde, And yow amende!"). The rioters, on the other hand, heap upon him such opprobrious epithets as "carl," "olde cherl," [20] and "false theef." In contrast to their grisly oaths ("And Cristes blessed body they to-rente"), the old man does not swear, but replies to their taunts with a quotation from Scripture. His piety, "curteisye," and humility are sharply distinguished from their blasphemy, "vileinye," and pride. He meets their threats of violence with "Debonairetee" and "Pacience or Suffrance." [21]

8. Finally, the old man's patient acceptance of the miseries of man's condition and his resignation to the divine will provide a striking contrast to the rioters' violent opposition to *la condition humaine* and their rash and impatient quest to slay death. Despite the old man's desire to die, he does not actually "seek" death.[22] The rioters, on the other hand, *are* engaged on a quest for death, and they "seek" him precisely because they do *not* wish to die.

III

To conclude, Chaucer's *senex* is quite intelligible on the literal level without resort to allegorical explanations. His chief significance is to be found in the ethical contrast he provides to Chaucer's characterization of the rioters. The encounter between them serves to emphasize such antithetical concepts as youth and age, folly and wisdom, avarice and *contemptus mundi*. As the moral opposite of the revellers, the old man lends additional proof to the Pardoner's theme.

He also serves a more practical end. Presumably the "lewd peple" who hear the Pardoner's sermon include both young and old. It is

[19] Cf. the behaviour of Life in Passus XX *Piers Plowman* XX(B) 142–50; and cf. Kellogg pp. 473–74 ("The essential contrast . . . is between living in accordance with 'goddeswille and living right at our owen wille' " etc.).

[20] In *The Parson's Tale*, the antithesis between "lordes" and "cherles" is discussed under the heading of *Avaricia* and related specifically to the theme of death.

[21] *The Parson's Tale* discusses these virtues under the heading *Remedium contra peccatum Ire*.

[22] *Pace* Sedgewick (Wagenknecht, p. 127).

worth reminding them that death comes to all and by various means. Hence he includes an additional detail in his *exemplum* of the young men who perish by *aventure*—an old man *ad mortis terminum*. He has no desire for the treasure or the "cheste" in his chamber. He can carry nothing to the grave except a "heyre clout." This demonstration of the uselessness of worldly possessions in "greet age" and in the face of death is calculated to serve the principal "entente" of the Pardoner's sermon —"for to make hem free To yeve her pens, and namely un-to me."

An Evaluation of the *Pardoner's Tale*

by Stephen A. Barney

> For though myself be a ful vicious man,
> A moral tale yet I yow telle kan,
> Which I am wont to preche for to wynne.
> Now hoold youre pees! My tale I wol bigynne.
>
> (459–62)

With these words the Pardoner completes his boastful and cynical account of the art of preaching for money. The tale which follows, and the more cynical demand for money which follows the tale, exemplify the Pardoner's art. If the tale is not precisely one of the Pardoner's sermons, it can be taken as a comparable piece of artifice, modified to suit the circumstances of the Canterbury pilgrimage and of Chaucer's reading or listening audience. The Pardoner's claim that "I stynge hym with my tonge smerte/ In prechyng" (413–14) is a claim likewise made on his audience and Chaucer's audience. Does his tale sting? Has it the power to move its audience? There seems to be a universal accord in the affirmative. Just as a corrupt priest can administer valid sacraments, so this bad man can tell a good tale. Criticism since Kittredge has offered subtle and ingenious readings of the tale and its surrounding material as *expression,* as a mode of characterization of the Pardoner himself, but little has been written about the quality of the tale itself—its interior harmonies and its capacities to elicit powerful response—beyond acknowledgement that it is good.

Several reasons may account for this silence, a silence we do not find in criticism of the *Knight's Tale* or the *Nun's Priest's Tale* or the *Clerk's Tale.* It may be thought that everyone can see why the tale is good. Critics may find the tale too short and simple to undergo their hard eye. Most important, the tale seems to have a source—and widespread analogues—but the exact source is unknown, so that Chaucer's unique contribution is impossible to assess. This last difficulty, with the exception of a few guesses, I have waived as, after all, not so considerable. The tale's virtues exist, no matter who is responsible for

them, and Chaucer included it in the *Canterbury Tales* so that we may
be permitted to view the tale in its significant context.

I propose that the *Pardoner's Tale* is good because it is eloquent, intelligent, significantly expressive, unified, and instructive. It is eloquent
because it maintains an ethos and a style which gather forces and affect
us throughout the tale; it is intelligent because it distinguishes things
which ought to be distinguished and combines what ought to be combined; it is significantly expressive because the character of its narrator
and the circumstances of its setting add to its meaning; it is unified in a
strict sense in that it is disposed in an orderly fashion, and all its parts
correspond and contribute to a single effect; and it is instructive because
it commands its audience to look at themselves and their world in a
new light.

Eloquence. The effect of the Pardoner's rhetoric can best be seen in
its dynamics—in the way the orator moves from topic to topic. The
reader of Chaucer commonly discovers that elements of the poems
which at first seem to be superfluous are in fact rhetorically strategic.
Perhaps the best-known case is the series of exempla: at first these
strings of old stories are lovable but dull, then they seem funny, then
thematically interesting, and finally, under the closest and most learned
reading, and under the broadest comparative view, they seem of the
quintessence of Chaucer's art. The principal excrescence in the manuscript fragment which contains the *Pardoner's Tale* is the *Physician's
Tale*; the second 'problem' is the homiletic proem on the tavern sins.

The *Physician's Tale* concerns a young lady, Virginia, who chooses
death rather than forced unchastity. The tale is horrible in two senses:
because it is badly told, and because it is gratuitously ugly in content.
There is no telling what Chaucer had in mind while he worked up the
tale, presumably with Livy and the *Romance of the Rose* before him,
laboring to increase the pathos of the heroine's plight much as he had
done in the *Clerk's Tale* and the *Man of Law's Tale*. Whatever Chaucer's initial opinion of his work, when he included it in the *Canterbury
Tales* he used it much as he had used other tales, which I shall call
'anti-tales,' either as foils for adjacent tales or as general parodies of
certain literary excesses of his time. The anti-tale is merely a special case
of the 'requital' principle in the *Canterbury Tales,* by which the
Knight's tale, for example, is answered by the Miller's. The best example of the foil arrangement is the *Monk's Tale,* interrupted and
sharply criticized on non-aesthetic grounds by the Knight and the Host,
and followed by the *Nun's Priest's Tale,* Chaucer's best, in which the
tragedy of fortune, so crudely handled by the Monk, is rendered in
high, comic, and ultimately more serious fashion by an intelligence of
the first order.

The *Pardoner's Tale* echoes the *Physician's Tale* at several points, as
we shall see; and I think there is little doubt that the pair are best

viewed together. The case I want to make here is that the Pardoner has
seen and makes use of the two major faults of the preceding tale. The
first is the imbalanced use of narrative materials. The Physician elabo-
rates at relatively great length on the virtues of Virginia, and on the
virtue and necessity of preserving innocent chastity itself, but leaves at
the periphery of the tale the really interesting matter: the character of
her father, and the operation of the legal system and its relation to the
public. A glance at Livy shows how, especially with regard to the latter
material, the story might better be told. In the Physician's version, the
intervention of "a thousand peple" who burst into court and save the
father immediately after he has beheaded his daughter is gratuitously
shocking. The auditor cannot help asking where were those people a
few moments before? Why did Virginius fail to appeal to them before?
Of course, this is melodrama and presumably an intentional effect of
the story; but I think it must render an audience speechless. Livy had
not presented this problem; Chaucer created it.

The second flaw in the *Physician's Tale* is the conclusion. Surely the
pathos of the tale, especially in this version, is for Virginia and the trial
of her virginity. Yet she is not mentioned in the closing lines. Instead
we are told "how synne hath his merite" (277)! To our surprise, the
final judgments on the villains, Apius and Claudius, turn out to be the
'moral' of the tale, and not the conflict between evils with which
Virginia and her father wrestle. Beware, the Physician warns, and forsake sin, for no man knows when God will smite, nor how the "worm
of conscience" will recoil from wicked life. This is conspicuous irrelevance, which the Pardoner notices and uses to his own ends.

I said the *Physician's Tale* would leave its audience speechless, but
I spoke of normal natures. Harry Bailly is a critic especially capable of
powerful emotional response and rapid, nearly simultaneous articula-
tion of his feelings. The first words after the *Physician's Tale* are, "Oure
Hooste gan to swere as he were wood;/ 'Harrow!' quod he . . ." (287–
88). There follows a shotgun blast of critical commentary. The falsity
of Apius and Claudius are berated; the cause of Virginia's death is
ascribed to the "yiftes of Fortune and of Nature," her beauty; the tale
is "pitous" (we have "pitee," "pitous," and "pitously" in twenty-odd
lines) so that the Host must hear a merry tale or else his "herte is lost"
(317). We might imagine the Pardoner thinking that pity runneth
soon in Harry's heart. The Host concludes with a request for enter-
tainment to the Pardoner, whom he calls "beel amy," with a not so
subtle glance at the Pardoner's effeminacy. The gentles, fearing that
the Pardoner will continue acting out his obviously assumed mask of
ribaldry, demand that he tell "som moral thing" (325).

I hope that this brief treatment of the matter which precedes the
Pardoner's Tale in the manuscript fragment (VI) shows how the Physician and the Host 'set up' the Pardoner and provide the initial

grounds for his eloquence. The sensitive audience has been affronted
in various ways by the Physician's literary failures, and the Pardoner
has been especially affronted by the Host's slur. He takes up the attack and does as well as a man in his condition can do, even though the
Host ultimately silences him; and the Knight, who seems to represent
"thise gentils," has to help the Pardoner reassume his composure.

The Pardoner responds to the *Physician's Tale* both by what he does
and what he does not do in his own tale. I shall need to anticipate some
arguments in order to summarize how he does so. First, as to motive: the
Physician says "the feend into his [Apius'] herte ran" (130) and taught
the judge the trick he needed to obtain Virginia; the Pardoner says of
the third rioter, "atte laste the feend oure enemy,/ Putte in his thought
that he sholde poyson beye" (844–45). It need scarcely be argued that
the introduction of the fiend as motive in the *Pardoner's Tale* is superfluous after all that has been said about the deadly effects of vice. Apius,
however, has been smitten by Virginia's beauty as suddenly as Troilus
by Criseyde's, and it apparently never occurs to him to behave by any
other counsel than the fiend's, who gets to his "herte" first, for reasons
which never come out. Secondly, we learn from the Physician that
Virginia was wont to flee the bad company who were "likely . . . to
treten of folye" (64); the Pardoner gives us the bad company itself and
thus avoids meeting the problem of poetic justice. Third, Virginia
twice refers to "grace" as she contemplates her dilemma, asking if there
will be "no grace . . . no remedye" (236) for herself, and reminding
her father that "Jepte" gave his daughter grace (here, time) to make her
complaint before he slew her (240). We shall see that the Pardoner
mingles the themes of grace and death more skillfully. Fourth, the Physician begins his description of Virginia with a curious prosopopoeia,
having Nature personified speak boastfully of her shaping and painting
of Virginia. This is the gift of Fortune and of Nature to which the Host
attributes the cause of Virginia's death. Again, we shall see how the
Physician's clumsy grasp of the truth about creaturely benefits—
especially clumsy since the Doctor's knowledge of causes is singled out
for special praise in the *General Prologue*—is transformed by the
Pardoner into an important theme of his tale. Fifth, the Physician's
conclusion that no one knows whom God will smite, rather stupid in
its context, is made the very occasion of the *Pardoner's Tale,* as the
rioters learn of the "privee theef men clepeth Deeth" (675). Sixth, the
Physician's moral, that "Heere may men seen how synne hath his
merite" (277), so hideously inappropriate to a tale of innocence de-
stroyed, has become the essential structural principle of the *Pardoner's
Tale.*

Finally, as far as I have seen, there is the matter of different uses of
rhetoric. The Physician had claimed of Virginia that "no countrefeted
termes hadde she" (51). The Host, producing an absurd list of pseudo-

medical terms in the link (urynals, jurdones, ypocras, galiones, letuarie, cardynacle, triacle), says, "I kan nat speke in terme" (311). We know from elsewhere in Chaucer of a distrust of jargon as part of a generalized antipathy toward fancy ideas and clericalism, as, for instance, in the prologue to the *Clerk's Tale*. The Host has told the Clerk, as later he tells the Pardoner, to tell a merry tale and has warned him from using "Youre termes, youre colours, and youre figures" (IV.16). Nature's speech is the principal 'rhetorical' ornament of the *Physician's Tale*, in medieval terms, being an extended figure of personification, and even including classical allusions. The Physician seems rather proud of it, ending it plumply with "Thus semeth me that Nature wolde seye" (29). It contains the terms "countrefete" (twice), "colour," and "figures." Nature uses these terms to describe her own work in creating as God's "vicaire general" (19), but the terms are all, as we see, especially rhetorical jargon, a point which I first noticed because of the close proximity of the phrase "countrefeted termes" (51) to describe Virginia's speech. In brief, my conjecture is this: the Physician accidentally connects Nature's skill at shaping with the skill of an orator, in a passage which is rhetorically deficient. The Host reemphasizes the issue with his parody of medical jargon in the link. The Pardoner then picks up the theme, but subtly. He uses Latin "to saffron with" his preaching; he has his bulls, his sealed patent, his allusions to popes, cardinals, patriarchs, and bishops, and especially his relics and his silver tongue —he is a kind of walking embodiment of rhetoric, the trappings and ornaments of his profession performing the functions of authorization and persuasion that terms and figures perform for an orator. As a speaker can use his craft to wrong effect, so can a pardoner use his office to wrong effect. The Pardoner's assertion that "I wol noon of the apostles countrefete" (447) indicates a rhetoric of behavior rather than a rhetoric of language. This is part of the reason why the Host's brutal response to the Pardoner's final offer is so effective: this Harry Bailly who so distrusts "termes" has seen through the Pardoner's superficies and has returned to the state of the purely physical such things as relics and masculinity, which are not purely physical when they are involved in the delicate magic of the Pardoner's art. The joke is that once the Pardoner finally launches into the tale proper (661–894) he uses almost no fancy rhetorical devices, with one exception, a personification, of which I shall make much later.

The first aspect of the Pardoner's eloquence, then, is his skill at listening. He seems to have caught in detail the flaws of the preceding tale and the inner meaning of the Host's response to it and to have turned them all to his own purposes. His confession of his methods, with its blunt exposure of the inner and outer motives of his preaching, comes as a shock after the fatuity and moral blindness of the *Physician's Tale*. In the Pardoner, the Canterbury pilgrims must see that if

they have to deal with vice, it will no longer be in the form of stupidity.
The prologue to the *Pardoner's Tale* is eloquent in a different sense:
it has the art of truth. No matter that we may see the Pardoner's
7 avarice as an audacious attempt to conceal his sexual inadequacy, he is
* still avaricious. Chaucer knew as well as Paul that sin is sin. As many
have observed, truth so baldly put is just as much an ornament as rhetorical lying. Again, at the end, the Pardoner's audacity is stripped away.

Finally, having looked under the rubric 'eloquence'—the eloquence
of responsiveness and the eloquence of truth—we should turn to the
eloquence of assertion within the tale itself. The tale is structured in
two ways which are characteristic of Chaucer. First is the bipartite
structure, or pace, of the tale, which might be labelled 'auctoritee'
followed by 'plot machine.' The Wife of Bath's prologue, which she
calls a tale, and her tale are the most famous examples of this scheme;
but we also find it in the talky beginnings and swift, eventful endings
of other tales: the *Miller's Tale,* the *Summoner's Tale,* the *Merchant's
Tale,* the *Nun's Priest's Tale,* and the *Physician's Tale* being outstand-
ing examples—and they include some of Chaucer's finest work. The
second structural characteristic is the efficiency of the plot machine, a
device which works so well for Chaucer that one might guess that he
was drawn with special delight to sources which contain this mechanism.

We expect the homily which fills the first part of the tale to be funny
yet serious (like the Wife of Bath's prologue) and to bear an indirect
but important relationship to the tale. We are disappointed. We might
think that the exempla of Attila, Stilboun, and Demetrius, or the interpretation of the original sin or the very energy devoted to the lesser sins,
are funny; but we know that it is the special kind of humor contemporary readers of Chaucer respond to with guilt, feeling fairly certain that Chaucer would not have seen the joke. The homily is pious
and deadly serious. There are signs of care in its composition as the
Pardoner turns from theme to theme, saying, "And now that I have
spoken of glotonye,/ Now wol I yow defenden hasardrye" (589–90) and
"Now wol I speke of othes false and grete" (629). The movement into
the homily is artful, as the pronouns of reference quietly shift from
the "they" of the rioters to the "we" and "you" of a preacher and his
audience, somewhere between lines 476 and 501. There is a little 'box'
structure of the sort we find elsewhere in Chaucer, in which the
Pardoner opens and closes a predicatorial topic on drunkenness with
the words "Sampsoun, Sampsoun!" (554, 572). This parallels in small
the large 'box' of the Pardoner's prologue, the phrase, "Radix malorum
est Cupiditas" (334, 426).

But the real force of the homily is its energy, its Chaucerian plenitude
and strenuousness. The images of vice the Pardoner chooses show men
distorted and strained by evil effort:

> How greet labour and cost is thee [wombe] to fynde!
> This cookes, how they stampe, and streyne, and grynde,
> And turnen substaunce into accident,
> To fulfille al thy likerous talent!
>
> (537–40)
>
> A lecherous thyng is wyn, and dronkenesse
> Is ful of stryvyng and of wrecchednesse.
> O dronke man, disfigured is thy face . . .
>
> (549–51)

The most striking device of the first, more energetic part of the homily is the one-line catalogue, the device which Milton and Pope use to similar effect, to suggest surfeit and chaotic bustle.[1] Chaucer's most famous example describes the materials that Absolon in the *Miller's Tale* used to clean his mouth: "With dust, with sond, with straw, with clooth, with chippes" (I.3748). Aside from the lines quoted in the first passage above, the Pardoner gives others in lines 465–66, 479, 534, 544, and 657.

It may be granted that the Pardoner's homily on the tavern sins is a tour de force of ordered disorder, urging the unattractiveness of sin, and by no means funny. Its relation to the rioters' plot is unusual. We and the pilgrim audience surely anticipate an indirect, and very likely comic connection. Instead, we have the simple arrangement: these men are vicious; here is the end of vice. The Pardoner keeps his eye steadily on the subject and even introduces into the homily some at first inexplicable references to death which serve to anticipate his plot: "Of whiche the ende is deeth, wombe is hir god!" (533); "he that haunteth swiche delices/ Is deed" (547–48); "For dronkenesse is verray sepulture/ Of mannes wit" (558–59); "Hasard is verray mooder of . . . manslaughtre" (591–93); "This fruyt cometh of the bicched bones two,/ . . . homycide" (656–57). These last three especially look odd until we reach the end, as we ask what have the tavern sins to do with homicide? But in spite of these overt connections, the homily is not a *sine qua non* for understanding the plot proper; it does not lay out themes like sovereignty and age (Wife of Bath) or scholarship and determinism (Nun's Priest) which open up the tale's significance. The relation, I think, is ethical only: the homily establishes an atmosphere and tone of disgust for vice and contempt for the vicious. The plot proper, astonishingly, comes as a considerable relief. We scarcely notice the dark setting, "this pestilence" (679), but of course it is there.

The eloquence of the plot is its elegance; it is plain and efficient and operates on life and truth like Occam's razor. It turns on two points: dramatic irony and ineluctable symmetry of judgment. The former I

---

[1] Cf. *Paradise Lost* II.948–50 and *Rape of the Lock* I.138.

wish to treat later. The symmetry of judgment consists in the generation of one motif out of another—hence plot 'machine'—as stupid
drunkenness begets a quest for death which begets greed for gold which
begets accidental revenge which begets death found. It is the mechanism
primarily characteristic of the fabliaux: the cry "Water!" in the *Miller's
Tale,* the "white thyng" in the moonlight in the *Reeve's Tale,* the
earnest oath in the *Friar's Tale,* the blindness in the *Merchant's Tale,*
the boastful, freeing word in the *Nun's Priest's Tale.* An apparently
extraneous but interesting element of plot comes suddenly as if by
magic to be essential, and theme (here, being death-bound in avarice)
becomes action (death in avarice). Inventing plots with this device
requires a special kind of imagination, that of a Fielding or a Dickens.
It was the imagination of the author of Genesis, who made the act of
eating the fruit of the Tree of Knowledge the knowledge itself. I think
there is no evidence that Chaucer was good at making up these stories,
but he was clearly interested in them, translating and rewriting and
weaving them into the texture of his *Canterbury Tales.* These plots
behave as the world properly behaves *sub specie aeternitatis,* turning
intangibles into tangibles and rendering justice at the end of time. I
have called this kind of plot 'magic,' but of course from the authorial
point of view it is that controlled magic which is better called intelligence.

Intelligence: this was our second reason for thinking the *Pardoner's
Tale* a good tale. We have noticed that the tale is eloquent, in its
response to the preceding tale, in the strikingly direct truthfulness of
its prologue, in the assertive rhetoric of the homiletic proem and the
elegant plot. The second pivot of the plot, its dramatic irony, I have
reserved for treatment until now, although this and all the other
'beauties' of the tale contribute in a general way to its eloquence.

We know more than the rioters do. We have seen the tavern vices
linked three times to death, and three times to homicide. We know
that death is not a person living in a village over a mile away or under
a tree in a grove. We know that the gold will not put the rioters "in
heigh felicitee" (787). We know, if we are clever, just before the end,
what the end will be. The Pardoner lends us, through his art, the
power of intelligence to discriminate between what the rioters see and
what is truly to be seen. When the worst of the rioters speaks after they
find the gold, and says, "My wit is greet" (778), we laugh. The rioters
are so incapable of understanding real value that they are glad of the
sight of the gold "For that the floryns been so faire and brighte" (774).
We are, in fact, maneuvered into a double vision of the events of the
tale, whereby we see what the rioters see but also see, from something
like a doomsday perspective, how things really are. Our double vision
operates in detail to unfold the meaning of the tale. The play on

Eucharistic transubstantiation in the lines already quoted about the cooks who "turnen substaunce into accident" (539) in their cooking may be taken as the key to this aspect of the tale: we are in a position to see things substantially while the rioters see accident only. The first figure of speech in the tale provides a correlative pair of terms: the rioters "doon the devel sacrifise/ Withinne that develes temple, in cursed wise" (469–70). This figure may derive from the puns in some medieval Latin verses on *taberna* (tavern) and *tabernaculum* (temple). To extend the metaphor, if the rioters' tavern is the devil's church, their whole vision of things is the devil's vision.

A telling distinction between the rioters' knowledge and ours lies in the accidental use of Biblical allusions by the characters in the tale. A rioter swears that "we wol sleen this false traytour Deeth" (699), and the narrator, in case we have missed the point, reiterates:

> And many a grisly ooth thanne han they sworn,
> And Cristes blessed body al torente—
> Deeth shal be deed, if that they may hym hente!
> (708–10)

We should here remember God's promise in Hosea 13 : 14, "I will deliver them out of the hand of death. I will redeem them from death: O death, I will be thy death; O hell, I will be thy bite"; and also Paul's use of the same logion: "O death, where is thy victory? O death, where is thy sting?" (I Cor. 15 : 55—Douay translation). But the rioters are killing Christ, the agent of life's victory, even as they set out to make death dead. A second allusion refers to the same chapter of Corinthians. Paul writes scornfully of those who do not believe in the resurrection, quoting Isaiah (22 : 13): "Let us eat and drink, for tomorrow we shall die" (I Cor. 15 : 32). The two rioters, having killed their companion, seem to echo these words: "Now lat us sitte and drynke, and make us merie,/ And afterward we wol his body berie" (883–84). The drink, of course, is poison.

Chaucer may also be recalling here a curiously analogous passage in the Book of Wisdom. The author is treating the themes of justice and death, and he quotes wicked men who do not reason right. They are aware of the brevity of life and say, "Come therefore, and let us enjoy the good things that are present, and let us speedily use the creatures as in youth. Let us fill ourselves with costly wine. . . . Let us . . . not . . . honour the ancient gray hairs of the aged." They are angry at the just man: "Let us therefore lie in wait for the just, because he . . . upbraideth us with transgressions of the law. . . . Let us condemn him to a most shameful death. . . . These things they thought, and were deceived: for their malice blinded them. . . . But by the envy of the devil, death came into the world: And they follow him that are of his side" (Wisdom 2 : 6, 7, 12, 20, 21, 24, 25). My elliptical quotation has improved my case, but even so this looks like the *Pardoner's Tale* if we substitute both the Old Man and the third rioter for the just man. In any case, the first chapters of Wisdom provide an apt commentary on our tale.[2]

The other two accidental Biblical allusions lend an apocalyptic cast to the 'substance' of the tale. The first, which is not certain, was noted by Robert Miller [see p. 67—ED.]. The Old Man wants death since he cannot have youth and complains, "Ne Deeth, allas! ne wol nat han my lyf" (727); during the locust plague of the fifth angel in the Apocalypse, John tells us, "And in those days men shall seek death, and shall not find it: and they shall desire to die, and death shall fly from them" (Apoc. 9 : 6). The second, which I think more likely, is the tavern boy's statement that "Ther cam a privee theef men clepeth Deeth" (675). This alludes to the famous group of apocalyptic logia which speak of the coming of the Son of Man as a thief in the night: "For yourselves know perfectly, that the day of the Lord shall so come, as a thief in the night" (I Thess. 5 : 2; and see Matt. 24 : 42; Luke 12 : 39; II Pet. 3 : 10; Apoc. 3 : 3 and 16 : 15). If the rioters had grasped these allusions, they might have known that judgment is at hand and that they are in the situation modern Biblical critics call realized eschatology.

The joke which begins the plot proper of the *Pardoner's Tale* is one of Chaucer's favorites, which might be called 'characterization by failure of imagination.'

The tavern boy explains to the rioters that an "old felawe" of theirs was slain by Death in the night. He warns the company to "be war of swich an adversarie" (682), as his "dame" had taught him. The taverner himself, misapprehending the statement, proceeds to generalize his sense that many have died recently during "this pestilence" and concludes that Death's "habitacioun" must be in the great village over a mile from the tavern. One of the rioters, in his cups, responds to this news as if it were a challenge—his bravado is the sole motive for the plot at this point—and says, "Is it swich peril with hym for to meete?" (693). The progression is from the dame's Christian lesson to the boy's possible misunderstanding to the taverner's utter misunderstanding to the rioters' action based on misunderstanding. What they misunderstand is the nature of personification, which is that the *accident* of the *substance* signified, in this case the *word* for *death,* can behave *in language* as if it were the substance itself, but not in reality. Personal names, "theef," "adversarie," "traytour," are apposed to the name, "Deeth," and the rioters assume the name is a person.

Their confusion, which Chaucer probably found in his source, cuts in two ways. First, obviously, it characterizes the rioters and taverner

[2] My colleague Leslie Brisman draws my attention to the maxim about the fruitful eunuch in the next chapter of Wisdom 3:14; and cf. also Isaiah 56:3 and Miller's article reprinted above, pp. 43–69.

as stupid. The Pardoner, who surely takes pride in his intelligence, may well be glancing at the offending taverner, Harry Bailly, in his present company. The other angle of incision, however, derives from a favorite medieval paradox, the basis of much classical allegory, that personifications like this one are real. The rioters do meet Death, not because it is a person, but because on a level of reality of which they are unaware, Death is victorious over them. Bertrand H. Bronson speaks of the movement into the tale and the rioters' misapprehension of death's nature as a movement toward miracle drama and allegory.[3] The landscape changes from the local and specific to the abstract and significant. The meeting point between the two worlds is the stile which the rioters are about to step over when they meet the Old Man; they enter just such a 'middle space' as Spenser's characters sometimes inhabit (as in *Faerie Queene* II.iv.32) in which moral states become physical actualities.

Finally, the tale's intelligence extends to the use of two terms, 'fortune' and 'grace.' The rioters address the Old Man, "What, carl, with sory grace!" (717), here an expletive of contempt; but later the same phrase describes the rioter who poisons his fellows (876). The Old Man complains that mother earth "wol nat do that grace" to give him death and burial (737). The rioter whose "wit is greet" says that "This tresor hath Fortune unto us yiven" (779), and, who would have thought "To-day that we sholde han so fair a grace?" (783). The rioters act without grace but think they have found it, as in fact they have—but it is the Old Man's version of grace. That gold is the gift of fortune is true, just as Virginia's beauty was the gift of Fortune and Nature in the Host's comment on the *Physician's Tale.* Yet the Pardoner is not telling a tale of Roman history but a moral tale. In his tale the scheme is providential, not fortunate. The rioters' apprehension of these terms corresponds to their apprehension of the value of gold, the meaning of the crooked path and the tree, the Biblical allusions, and the personification, Death. The tale works in a way analogous to the method of satire. When we are shown failure of imagination and insensitivity to large perspectives, we readers perforce assume the large perspective ourselves and become, while we partake of the tale, instruments of divine vision and justice. We are Providence, and we keep watch for the thief who comes suddenly in the night.

The *Pardoner's Tale* is significantly expressive. Whatever the Pardoner's physical condition, his fellow pilgrims treat him as effeminate. In place of the obvious signs of masculinity, the Pardoner has his tongue, which goes "yerne" (398), which is "smerte" in stinging (413), which spits out venom (421), and which the narrator describes as 'well-

[3] Bertrand H. Bronson, *In Search of Chaucer* (Toronto: University of Toronto Press, 1960), pp. 101–3.

filed' in the *General Prologue* (I.712); he has also his wallet stuffed
with relics and "bretful of pardoun," mentioned three times in the
General Prologue and once in the epilogue to the tale (920). His tongue
and wallet, the tools of his trade, behave like phallic symbols.[4] The
obscene conclusion of the *Romance of the Rose,* for example, treats a
wallet as a scrotum. When the Pardoner invites the Host to kiss his
relics and suggests that he "Unbokele anon thy purs" (945)—for money,
not, as usually, for a tale—Harry's references to the Pardoner's "breech"
and "coillons" show that he responds to the Pardoner in these sexual
terms. The Host is the very figure of masculinity which the Pardoner
envies. His wish that the Pardoner be castrated is the final blow, and
the Pardoner's tongue emphatically ceases its work:

> "Lat kutte hem of, I wol thee helpe hem carie;
> They shul be shryned in an hogges toord!"
> This Pardoner answerde nat a word;
> So wrooth he was, no word ne wolde he seye.
>
> (954-57)

As long as Chaucer's work survives, the Pardoner will be "This" Pardoner at the end of his tale, a man set at a distance from us, and the
word "word" will be associated with him through its rhyme, "toord."

The Pardoner offers first his tale, then his relics; from his point of
view they are gifts of the same order. He gives as best he can the impression that *he* can see beneath the accidents of narrative art and
sacred object to the real substance, his desire for gain. The Host's
criticism of the tale is for once forestalled by the Pardoner's rapid
patter. He can only reply to the relics, obviously specious, with proper
disgust and anger.

It remains to determine our final response to the tale. One way to
consider this question is to consider the fourth excellence of the tale,
its unity. This is comprised of the elaborate scheme of corresponding
duplicities which the tale and its teller present. The Physician tells his
tale, which fails to penetrate to true causes, with good intentions; the
Pardoner tells his more penetrating tale with bad intentions. The Pardoner confesses to avarice and blindness to the final judgment; his tale
condemns avarice and opens our eyes to the end of things. The Pardoner fills his audience with disgust for vice in his homily; he fills
them with disgust for his vicious person in the epilogue. The tale care-

---

[4] These remarks derive from a suggestion by Professor Stephen Manning that the
Pardoner's tongue is phallic. Chaucer may have thought to associate relics with
genitalia because of some usages in the *Romance of the Rose.* There "coilles" or
"coillons" are associated with "reliques" (ll. 7081–82, Langlois ed.), and the word
"bourses" (wallets) is given as a euphemism for genitalia (l. 7143). The Tobler-
Lommatzsch *Altfranzösisches Wörterbuch* cites this second reference as evidence for
a figurative sense of "borse" as "Hodensack" (scrotum), and lists one reference from
outside the *Romance of the Rose.*

fully distinguishes accidental value from substantial value, irate, avaricious and gluttonous language from Biblical language, personification from spiritual reality; but the Pardoner in himself confuses all things, as liar and truth-teller at once. Very different are the analogues to the tale, in which saintly or divine figures of high authority provide the framework of meaning.

There are many ways of looking at these fusing, paralleling, contradicting, complicated relationships. Harry Bailly's way is to reduce all to a turd; the Knight's way is to insist on the continuance of the game. I think Chaucer is very serious in providing these more or less limited judgments from fellow pilgrims. The poet poses a question which—as the prologue and epilogue to the *Parson's Tale* show—was on his mind: whether this business of writing good literature, or telling good tales, makes any sense at all from the doomsday perspective or the perspective of natural reason. The Pardoner is an example of a literary artist who uses his craft according to the mutable realm of Fortune, with his eye cast to the earth.

The *Pardoner's Tale* is instructive. If we have any imagination, any power to make distinctions and draw analogies, we must look at last at ourselves when we finish reading the tale and wonder what we have been doing. If the tale alone is a true analogy to the world, then the rhetoric of art will be duplicated in the history of events, and our fictional experience of vitality and justice will be made real. If the tale in its setting, in the mouth of the Pardoner in the *Canterbury Tales,* is true, we may be exercising our imagination to no end or, like the Pardoner, to mean ends. All that beauty and energy, of the Pardoner's and maybe of Chaucer's, is for nothing. The magical things which can happen in a tale may have no counterpart in the world. The tale is a trial of faith.

"That We May Leere Som Wit"

by Janet Adelman

The Pardoner casts his spell over modern readers of the *Canterbury Tales* as surely as he did over the original pilgrims. But the very brilliance of his spell has tended to divert attention away from the structure of his prologue and tale and its place in the framework of the whole pilgrimage. The figure of the Pardoner himself, his mysterious confession and the apparent outburst of sincerity at the end of his sermon; the macabre brilliance of the inset *exemplum;* the identity of the Old Man—these have generally been the preoccupations of readers and critics alike. My attempt in this essay will consequently be to draw a few thematic connections and to suggest their relevance to some of the aesthetic questions posed by the tale: questions both of its own form and of its relation to its teller, its audience, and ultimately to the author of all the tales. I shall be concerned with the structure of the tale particularly insofar as it is a game of wit. For it is part of the Pardoner's bag of tricks that he simultaneously satisfies the gentles' request for "som moral thyng" and the Host's request for "som myrthe or japes." Despite its moral solemnity, the tale is a brilliantly constructed comedy, simultaneously a parody of the very truths it purports to be about and a joke in which we are never quite sure of the butt. In discussing this structure, I do not hope to reduce the tale to any formula which can account for its false starts and peculiarities of emphasis;[1] indeed, the very raggedness of its external structure seems to

---

[1] These peculiarities of structure are everywhere apparent. Many of the Pardoner's *exempla* for his pet sins are curiously indecisive: what will his audience learn from Lemuel or Stilboun? The announced subject of the tale is cupidity, and the Pardoner begins a tale which illustrates its dangers perfectly; but he immediately interrupts the tale with a long diatribe against gluttony, hasardry, and swearing—sins which are not immediately related to cupidity. D. W. Robertson's attempt to sort out part of this confusion is brilliant: he suggests that gluttony, gambling, and swearing are in fact subdivisions of *cupiditas*. [See the last selection in this volume —ED.] But even Robertson is forced to acknowledge that the Pardoner's explication of the sins is not as tidy as his own: "In the sermon itself, these transgressions are not ordered in accordance with any set principles, or at least the principles are not made explicit, probably because Chaucer did not wish the Pardoner to seem aware of

me an important aspect of its final effect. We never know quite where the Pardoner is going; and insofar as we are all unknowing participants in his game, our uneasiness is part of the point.

The Pardoner's prologue and tale follow immediately after the *Physician's Tale*; the Pardoner is in fact called upon to supply a remedy for the dolors of that tale. The Host describes his reaction to the Physician's tale in mock-medical jargon and then prescribes ale or a merry tale as a cure for his disease. The Host's medical joke reinforces the connection between the two physicians: the doctor of the body and the supposed doctor of the spirit. Moreover, both of these physicians tell tales about death: in the Physician's tale, death of the body is apparently necessary to avoid death of the spirit; in the Pardoner's tale, death of the spirit is the cause of death of the body. We move, that is, from a tale of physical death to one of spiritual death. Death as in the Pardoner's tale is quite beyond the Physician's art. Though the immediate cause of the rioters' death is poison, the ultimate cause is curable only by Christ, "oure soules leche" (916). The implicit contrast between the two kinds of death and the two kinds of physicians suggests that confusion of physical with spiritual which is at the heart of the *Pardoner's Tale*. Throughout the tale, we find the attempt to cure spiritual diseases by physical means, cures as ludicrously inadequate as the Host's. When the rioters hear that Death has slain a "felawe" of theirs, they arrange themselves in a secular trinity and swear to kill Death:[2]

> Herkneth, felawes, we thre been al ones;
> Lat ech of us holde up his hand til oother,
> And ech of us bicomen otheres brother,
> And we wol sleen this false traytour Deeth. *But death is not a spiritual disease*
> He shal be slayn, he that so manye sleeth,
> By Goddes dignitee, er it be nyght!
>
> (696–701)

Their literal-minded desire to kill death is comic; but at the same time, their desire to cure death by killing him physically is a symptom of their disease. Their vow that "Deeth shal be deed" (710) suggests a literal substitution for Christ's triumph over death; ultimately, only "oure soules leche" can cure death. It is in fact their desire to seek a

---

the implications of what he says for himself." Perhaps Chaucer expected us to perceive a scheme which he carefully obscures; but in fact it seems more likely that we are all meant to be somewhat confused by the Pardoner's exposition.

[2] The repetition of "felawe" throughout the tale emphasizes their perverted fellowship, perhaps parodic of the "felaweshipe" of the pilgrims (I.26, 32). The word occurs at ll. 672, 696, 810, 846, 878, 887. The repetition of "brother" or "brethren" at ll. 704, 777, and 808 intensifies this emphasis.

physical cure for death which kills them. The Old Man who sends the three to their deaths illustrates in his own person their disastrous confusion between cure and ailment: in his physically eternal life, he embodies the very cure for which they seek; and this 'cure' is itself the disease from which he seeks release.[3] Moreover, the *exemplum* of the rioters explicates in narrative form the Pardoner's own disease: his substitution of his physical cures for spiritual salvation. The Pardoner reminds us constantly that Christ "bought" us with his "precious" blood.[4] But in his mouth the words take on a distinctly commercial tinge: he will sell us his own pardon for a price. Even in his descriptions of sin, the Pardoner deftly substitutes physical for spiritual diseases: it is the vomit of the drunken man that makes him loathesome. In place of baptism, he offers to secure for his audience magical water which will cure diseases of livestock. And if any of his churchly audience accepts these remedies, he succumbs to the same disease that infects his pardoner.[5]

The substitution of physical for spiritual is the thematic concern of the tale insofar as it is an expression of the *cupiditas* of the epigraph: for *cupiditas* in its fullest sense is just this substitution of the things of the world for the things of God. The theological implications of this substitution have been explicated by several commentators;[6] I am here chiefly concerned with the aesthetic implications. For the concept of *cupiditas* gives the tale its aesthetic as well as its moral shape. Throughout the tale, we encounter literal versions of spiritual facts: the multiplying of "beestes and . . . stoor" (365) rather than of either human generations or of good deeds; the earthly treasure hidden under the tree rather than the treasure of eternal life found on the cross; the poison which is "the montance of a corn of whete" (863) rather than the mustard seed which is like the kingdom of heaven. These ver-

---

[3] If the Old Man whose mother is earth is allied to St. Paul's first man, Adam, who is "of the earth, earthy" (I Corinthians 15:47), then his punishment has that ironic appropriateness so common in this tale. For his devotion to the body, he is given physically eternal life; his punishment is in fact a literalization of his spiritual disease. In this sense, he is like those spiritually dead in hell: "They shullen folwe deeth, and they shul nat fynde hym; and they shul desiren to dye, and deeth shal flee fro hem" (*Parson's Tale*, X.216).

[4] Both words occur frequently in the tale in reference to Christ's pardon. "Bought": cf. ll. 501, 503, 766, and 902. "Precious": cf. ll. 651, 902. The word "precious" is used twice to refer to Christs blood; hence its use at l. 775 to refer to the treasure is pointedly ironic.

[5] The Pardoner's sin is, of course, simony; and as the Parson points out in his tale, "bothe he that selleth and he that byeth thinges espirituels, been cleped Symonials' (X.781).

[6] Robert P. Miller's essay, "Chaucer's Pardoner, the Scriptural Eunuch, and *The Pardoner's Tale*," deals most fully with the theological implications of *cupiditas*. We note many of the same details, though our uses of them are different. [This essay is reprinted here, pp. 43–69—ED.]

sions mock their spiritual equivalents by imitating their literal form rather than their spiritual content, by aping rather than truly imitating. In this sense, they are all deadly parodies, literal imitations which mock by their very absence of spirit. Just as the rioters' mock-trinity is a parody of the true Trinity and the Old Man's living death a parody of eternal life, the Pardoner himself as eunuch is a parody of the true eunuch for Christ.[7] If the oak tree is literally the *radix malorum*, the tree which brought death into Eden, it is also a parody of the Cross, the true tree with death at its foot. This aping of the letter rather than the spirit is not merely a literary device; it is characteristic of *cupiditas* itself. There is, in fact, a firm philosophic basis for the representation of evil as a false imitation of good: whether in the Platonic doctrine that man will choose evil only when he mistakes it for good, or in St. Augustine's assertion that

> All who desert you [God] and set themselves up against you merely copy you in a perverse way; but by this very act of imitation they only show that you are the Creator of all nature.[8]

In this sense, *cupiditas is* false imitation: the moral and aesthetic designs of the tale are one.

Insofar as parody is characteristic of its structure, the tale depends on a continual process of analogy. Details are often insignificant except insofar as they are recognized as parodic literalizations of the spirit: thus it would not matter that the Pardoner likened himself to a dove beckoning his parishioners (397) if we did not remember the image of the Holy Ghost. Insofar as parody works only when it thus points us toward the thing parodied, the parodic analogies function to remind us of everything that the Pardoner's distorting vision excludes. In this sense, the tale tends always to break down its own boundaries and, in effect, to point out the limitations of its teller. That is, the analogies reflect outward not only toward the spiritual facts which the Pardoner mocks, but also toward the Pardoner and his audience. By the end, the process of parody implicates us all. There are, I think, two images central to this process of analogy: that of the rioters and their poisoned wine, and that of the artist and his audience.

In the course of his diatribe against gluttony, the Pardoner describes cooking as a process in which spirit is literally transformed into matter:

> Thise cookes, how they stampe, and streyne, and grynde,
> And turnen substaunce into accident!
>
> (538–39)

[7] See Miller for an explication of the theological significance of the Pardoner's disability.

[8] St. Augustine, *Confessions*, II.6, trans. R. S. Pine-Coffin (Baltimore: Penguin Books, 1961), p. 50.

In cooking, servant to gluttony, the essence itself becomes all accident.[9] But it is the central mystery of the Eucharist that the essence of the bread and wine become Christ's flesh and blood, while their physical properties or accidents remain unchanged.[10] By his scholastic joke, the Pardoner makes the art of cookery into a parody of the Eucharist. Gluttons are the "enemys of Cristes croys" (532); if Christ's communion is life, the gluttonous communion is death. But this is precisely the communion which the rioters celebrate at the end of their pilgrimage. The youngest of the three is sent to town for "breed and wyn" (797); when he returns, the others "ryve hym thurgh the sydes tweye" (828) as Christ was riven. The remaining "felawes" then celebrate their communion with the poisoned wine:

> "Now lat us sitte and drynke, and make us merie,
> And afterward we wol his body berie."
> And with that word it happed hym, par cas,
> To take the botel ther the poyson was,
> And drank, and yaf his felawe drynke also,
> For which anon they storven bothe two.
>
> (883–88)

The rioters' pilgrimage to slay death begins in a tavern; and the tavern's wine is its inevitable conclusion. Like gluttony, of which it is a species, drunkenness is itself deadly: the Pardoner tells us that it is the "verray sepulture/ Of mannes wit and his discrecioun" (558–59), and he should know. Even the felawe whom the three swear to avenge "was yslayn to-nyght,/ Fordronke" (673–74). The final death by poison is only the explication of the death already implicit in the wine, the false sacrament. This sacrament of wine becomes in effect the type of all the substitutions of literal for spiritual: as a deadly parody of the Eucharist, it stands at the center of the parodic structure of the tale.

[9] The word "accident" suggests neatly the relationship between *cupiditas* and Fortune. The rioters drink the poisoned wine "par cas" (885); but in this tale there are no accidents. Man is at the mercy of Fortune's accidents only when he cares too much for the accidents of matter; *cupiditas* is, in one sense, the willing subjection to the realm of Fortune. Even the agent of their death, the one sent into town, is chosen by lots. The Host warns in the link between the Physician's and Pardoner's tales that "yiftes of Fortune and of Nature/ Been cause of deeth to many a creature" (295–96); but the rioters do not realise that they have found in their gift of Fortune (779) the death for which they sought. Those who live according to Fortune will die according to Fortune: par cas. Indeed, the poisoned wine is an accident in precisely the same sense as the rioters' death is par cas: one accident is contingent upon the other.

[10] According to F. N. Robinson's note, "Substance and accident are used in their philosophical senses, the real essence of a thing, and the outward qualities . . . by which it is apprehended. . . . Chaucer can hardly have used this phrase without thinking of the current controversy about the Eucharist" (*Works of Geoffrey Chaucer*, p. 730).

As we begin his tale, the Pardoner takes pains to remind us that it is the *exemplum* in his sermon: the rioters' tavern and the false pilgrimage it initiates are themselves set within the context of the church. But this church is set within the larger context of the tavern: the Pardoner delivers his mock-sermon only after he has stopped for a drink.[11] The poisoned wine and the true sacrament, the tavern and the church: these are the alternatives which determine the structure of the tale. For in one sense, the structure is that of concentric circles formed by these alternating contexts: the rioters' pilgrimage and sacrament; the tavern from which they start; the church in which the Pardoner preaches his sermon; the tavern at which he drinks. Nor does the process of analogy stop here. For the Pardoner's tavern is a way-stop on a pilgrimage which itself began in a hostelry, a pilgrimage from the Tabard to Canterbury; and from this perspective, the poisoned wine of the Pardoner's tale has chilling implications for the pilgrims. The rioters' pilgrimage to slay death is in fact analogous to that pilgrimage to St. Thomas a Becket, "that hem hath holpen whan that they were seeke" (I.18). And there are disturbing similarities between the two, similarities which suggest that our pilgrimage may itself be a false analogy for the "parfit glorious pilgrymage" (X.50). Like the rioters, our pilgrims set out from the tavern in the morning. Before they have left the Tabard, they place themselves under the guidance of "oure Host," Harry Bailly:

> . . . We wol reuled been at his devys
> In heigh and lough; and thus by oon assent
> We been acorded to his juggement.
> And therupon the wyn was fet anon;
> We dronken, and to reste wente echon.
>
> (I.816–20)

If the wine is any indication, they are indeed accorded to his judgment. But however excellent he may be as master of ceremonies, a tavern-keeper is no fit guide for a pilgrimage. The end of the pilgrims' journey is the host of the Eucharist, hardly the host they have just accepted. If the pilgrims substitute the remedies of the tavern for those of the

---

[11] It does not matter whether we imagine the tale as told actually in the tavern or merely after reenforcement from the tavern: this tale alone is placed in such close proximity to the tavern. Chaucer takes pains to emphasize this proximity: the Pardoner twice before his prologue (321–22 and 328) and once at its conclusion (456) calls attention to his drink. Moreover, the Pardoner's desire to stop "heere at this alestake" and "bothe drynke, and eten of a cake" (321–22) recalls the description of his friend the Sommoner in the *General Prologue*: "A gerland hadde he set upon his heed/ As greet as it were for an ale-stake./ A bokeleer hadde he maad hym of a cake" (I.666–68). Both images suggest a complex parody of the communion; the Summoner in particular seems to be wearing his own version of the whole armor of Christ.

church, the rioters' communion will become theirs: it is no wonder
that they are uncomfortable when the Pardoner reminds them that
they, like the rioters, may die by accident.

The *exemplum* ultimately implicates the entire pilgrimage by analogy. Safe in their position as audience, the pilgrims attend to the tale
—until that moment when they discover that they are not only its audience but also its subject. At the point when the Pardoner turns his
sales pitch toward the pilgrims, it becomes clear that the joke is on
them. Nor does the insult end here. If the tale of the rioters mocks their
status as pilgrims, the Pardoner's ignorant church audience mocks their
status as audience. Initially the Pardoner's confession carefully sepa-
rates the pilgrims from that audience of gulls to whom he preaches:
"Lordynges . . . in chirches whan I preche . . ." (329). He freely admits that he tricks this audience by telling them "an hundred false
japes" (394) and "ensamples many oon/ Of olde stories" (435–36). But
in the course of his old story, the distinction between the pilgrims
and the church audience is blurred: by the time he addresses the church
audience as "lordynges" (573), the two audiences have become one. His
spell is so successful that we come to the end of his act—"And lo, sires,
this I preche" (915)—with a start. As the pilgrims listen to his tale,
they become in effect the "lewed peple" (437), subject to his pitch. He
will offer them the security of his pardon just as he offers it to his audience of gulls. Moreover, the Pardoner's *leger de main* with these audiences implicates us as well as the pilgrims. Part of our discomfort when
he turns to the pilgrims and offers them his pardon comes, I think,
from our sense that he has violated one of the conventions that sepa-
rates him from us, that he has in effect moved *us* one degree closer to
the reality of the tale. We are threatened with the loss of our cherished
standing as uninvolved spectators; we too may become his dupes.
      But in this tale of shifting analogies, it is never clear for long who
is the butt of the joke. The Host asks the Pardoner for "myrthe or
japes" and is repaid with the final joke at his own expense. But the
Pardoner's joke on the Host backfires notoriously. The tale is in fact
filled with jokes that backfire, and the jokes are all of a particularly
deadly kind. The tale is first of all a joke on the rioters. The Old Man
plays a simple trick on them; and their response when they find the
gold—"no lenger thanne after Deeth they soughte" (772)—is chillingly
comic. But the success of his trick depends ultimately on their willingness to trick themselves. The worst of the rioters plans to stab the
youngest, while the other "strogelest with hym as in game" (829). And
just as the rioters' game is deadly, so is the Pardoner's: for, ultimately,
the joke is on him. It is part of the peculiar nightmare of this tale that
the Pardoner's little joke catches him unawares just as surely as it
catches the pilgrims.

The Pardoner's art is preeminently one in which audience participation is necessary: it succeeds only insofar as his audience becomes his dupes. We do indeed hate art which has such palpable designs on us. But if the tale redefines the affective boundary of art, it also redefines the genetic. In his boast that his "entente is nat but for to wynne,/ And nothyng for correccioun of synne" (403–4), the Pardoner inverts the moral function not only of his sermons but of all art, directing it not toward the use of his audience but toward himself. And just as he inverts this relationship between artist and audience, he inverts the relationship between teller and tale. The Pardoner is in effect an early opponent of the intentional fallacy, positing with disconcerting clarity the irrelevance of intention: "For certes, many a predicacioun/ Comth ofte tyme of yvel entencioun" (407–8). He claims that his art is autonomous, totally separate from his own character: "For though myself be a ful vicious man,/ A moral tale yet I yow telle kan" (459–60). But he is in fact implicated by his own tale even as he claims its autonomy. His drunkenness and cupidity make the rioters' pale by comparison; nor does he seem to recognize his own spiritual death in the Old Man. The tale is moral not in spite of his viciousness but because of it. Ultimately, he is the most persuasive *exemplum* for his own tale even in his claim that it is autonomous, an exercise that he knows "by rote" (332). For this very claim suggests the separation of words from matter, of letter from spirit. His separation of tale from teller is in fact a type of the false swearing he warns against, parodying not only the true function of the artist but also all true uses of the Word.

The Pardoner uses his wit to beguile his church audience and the pilgrims; but finally he beguiles himself. He is the most intellectually arrogant of the pilgrims, contemptuous of the "lewed peple" to whom he preaches and ultimately of all of the pilgrims. But finally his intellectual pride is misplaced: he seems again and again to miss the point of his own elaborate structure. For all his wit, the Pardoner does not know what is important and what is not. And it is precisely his pride in his intellect, his claim to be exempt from his own moral categories, that tricks him. In his disastrous perversion of the true ends of wit, he himself is the "verray sepulture/ Of mannes wit and his discrecioun." The Pardoner's sin—his use of wit to serve himself rather than God— is the most deadly in the tale; and it is the sin of which the Pardoner, for all his intellectual prowess, is ignorant.

Finally, the Pardoner's game of false wit implicates not only the pilgrims and the Pardoner himself, but also the teller of all the tales. The pilgrimage begins in the morning with the sense of a world freshly created and ends in the afternoon with the sense of the shadow of death; it begins with the new earth of Genesis and ends with the holy city of Revelation. As we approach that holy city, we encounter the

corrective figure of the Parson, the last of the pilgrims. His tale is a
sermon, in fact the true sermon of which the Pardoner's is the false
copy:[12] it shows us the way to pardon through contrition rather than
through the Pardoner's mechanical means. And in his prologue, the
Parson reasserts the true source and use of wit; he prays that

> . . . Jhesu, for his grace, wit me sende
> To shewe yow the wey, in this viage,
> Of thilke parfit glorious pilgrymage
> That highte Jerusalem celestial.
>
> (X.48–51)

Our fictive pilgrimage itself is only an imitation of that true pilgrimage; and in the light of that truth, the Parson has no patience with
fiction. The game of fiction was invented by the Host to pass the time
on the way from the tavern to our journey's end;[13] and as we approach
that end, the game must be broken.[14] The Parson refuses to participate
in the Host's game:

> Thou getest fable noon ytoold for me;
> For Paul, that writeth unto Thymothee,
> Repreveth hem that weyven soothfastnesse,
> And tellen fables and swich wrecchednesse.
>
> (X.31–34)

[12] Many of the Pardoner's phrases are echoed in the Parson's sermon. The Parson,
like the Pardoner, blames the fall on gluttony: "this synne corrumped al this world,
as is wel shewed in the synne of Adam and of Eve" (X.819; cf. VI.504ff.: "Corrupt
was all this world for glotonye . . ."). This arrangement is closely associated with St.
Paul in the *Parson's Tale,* as it is in the Pardoner's: "Looke eek what seith Seint
Paul of Glotonye:/ 'Manye,' seith Saint Paul, 'goon, of whiche I have ofte seyd to
yow, and now I seye it wepynge, that been the enemys of the croys of Crist; of
which the ende is deeth, and of whiche hire wombe is hire god" (X.819–20; cf.
VI.529–33). Perhaps the most startling echo of the Pardoner is in the Parson's diatribe against the sins of the tongue: "But lat us go now to thilke horrible sweryng
of adjuracioun and conjuracioun, as doon thise false enchauntours or nigromanciens
in bacyns ful of water, or in a bright swerd, in a cercle, or in a fir, or in a shulder-
boon of a sheep" (X.603). We remember the Pardoner's "sholder-boon/ Which that
was of an hooly Jewes sheep" (VI.350–51), that magical relic by which he conjures.
The Pardoner's use of the word is in fact a kind of necromancy, in opposition to
the Parson's true use of the word.
[13] The rioters commit the Pardoner's three pet sins in the course of the tale: they
swear a false oath when they establish their trinity; they are gamblers when they
cast lots; and they are gluttons as they drink the wine. It is curious that the pilgrims
commit the same sins in little as they establish the Host's game: they swear to
obey the Host; they draw cuts to see who will tell the first tale; and their prize is a
free supper.
[14] According to Revelation 21:27, nothing shall enter into the holy city "that
defileth, neither whatsoever worketh abomination, or maketh a lie."

But all fiction must in some sense "weyven soothfastnesse"; it is all in some measure a form of false swearing.[15] And true wit will renounce fiction along with the other sins of the tongue. In this sense, the Pardoner's lies are only an extreme instance of the problem inherent in the game of fiction itself. And insofar as the Pardoner is a false imitation of the Parson, Chaucer himself is implicated in the game. At the final moment he achieves what the Pardoner could never achieve: the realization that he is not exempt from his own moral categories. If the pilgrimage begins in fiction, it ends in truth: in place of the fictive narrator of the *General Prologue,* we have the unmasked voice of the poet in the *Retraction.* It is not only the Parson but the poet himself who breaks the game of fiction: Chaucer's voice seems to merge with the Parson's as he prays for that "grace of verray penitence, confessioun and satisfaccioun" (X.1090) of which the Parson had preached. In his own person, he acknowledges both the true use of wit and its true source:

> Now preye I to hem alle that herkne this litel tretys or rede, that if ther be any thyng in it that liketh hem, that therof they thanken our Lord Jhesu Crist, of whom procedeth al wit and al goodnesse (X.1081).

Like the Pardoner's game, Chaucer's game of fiction finally implicates us. The Pardoner at the end of his tale tells his audience that Christ's pardon is best, "I wol yow nat deceyve" (918). For a moment, the Pardoner disavows his deception; but immediately afterward he asks the pilgrims to participate in the deception by buying his pardon. At the end of all the tales, Chaucer too disavows his deception: but he asks us to participate in the disavowal.

> Wherefore I biseke yow mekely, for the mercy of God, that ye preye for me that Crist have mercy on me and foryeve me my giltes;/ and namely of my translacions and enditynges of worldly vanitees (X.1084-85.)

But as audience, how do we feel when we are asked to pray for forgiveness of Chaucer's sins of fiction? Most of us have enjoyed the tales "that sownen into synne" (X.1086) more than the sinless ones; and we are uncomfortable to be implicated in Chaucer's renunciation of them. If the Pardoner's audience is irritated when it is asked to participate in the fiction, we are irritated when we are asked to participate in the truth. Soothfastness may be the goal of the pilgrimage; but what do we do while we are still on the way? We find ourselves nostalgic for fiction even after it has been disavowed; and our reading of the end of the *Canterbury Tales* does not change our reading of the tales along

---

[15] In the Parson's diatribe against swearing, he condemns also that form of lying which "comth of delit for to lye, in which delit they wol forge a long tale, and peynten it with alle circumstaunces, where al the ground of the tale is fals" (X.610).

the way. The Host, the Wife of Bath, and the Pardoner are better travelling companions than the Parson; compared to the richness of fiction, soothfastness itself will seem impoverished. Our position as readers caught between fiction and soothfastness is analogous to that of the pilgrims, caught between the tavern and the church. By the process of analogy, we are forced to experience their tension. And, like the pilgrims, we know which we are supposed to choose; but we also know what we like.

PART TWO

View Points

George Lyman Kittredge: from *Chaucer and His Poetry*

The exemplum which the sermon embodies is one of the best in the world, and comes from the Orient, where it is still in popular circulation. It tells the fate of the three revellers who sally forth to kill Death. I have already mentioned it, in my first lecture, where I spoke of the skill that Chaucer shows in the resolution after the climax. Further detail is unnecessary, for the tale is very familiar to modern readers. Still, I must dwell for a moment on one passage, which affords a remarkable illustration of effective reticence.

The aged wayfarer whom the three rioters encounter, and whom they treat with such rudeness, is undoubtedly Death in person. But Chaucer does not say so. He describes him as an old, old man who cannot die. This old man directs the rioters to the tree under which lies the fatal treasure, and passes on his way, with the grimly significant remark, "I moot go thider as I have to go." Death, of course, has his own affairs to attend to during this pestilence season, and the rioters are his, safe enough: they have but to follow his directions, and covetousness will provide for that! And so the tragedy proceeds without delay to its inexorable conclusion.

The Pardoner knows his sermon by heart (he has told us as much), and its momentum carries him beyond the point at which, on this particular occasion, he ought to have stopped,—carries him, indeed, so far that he appends his customary summons to come up to the chancel, make offering to the relics, and receive absolution. This summons is quite in order when he is preaching to the villagers in some country church, but now he realizes, when once it is uttered, that it is inopportune enough in the present company, who have no illusions about either his relics or himself. And so he cynically reminds his fellow-travellers of what he told them at the outset,—that he is merely giving them a specimen of his pulpit oratory: "And lo, sires, thus I preche!"

Then, suddenly, unexpectedly, without an instant's warning, his cynicism falls away, and he utters the solemn words: "May Christ, the physician of our souls, grant you His pardon, for that is better than mine! I will not deceive you, though I get my living by fraud!"

> I yow assoile by myn heigh power,
> Yow that wol offre, as clene and eek as cleer
> As ye were born.—And lo! sires, thus I preche.
> And Jhesu Crist, that is oure soules leche,
> So graunte yow his pardoun to receyve;
> For that is best—I wol yow nat deceyve!
>
>   (913–18)

The Pardoner has not always been an assassin of souls. He is a renegade, perhaps, from some holy order. Once he preached for Christ's sake; and now, under the spell of the wonderful story he has told and of recollections that stir within him, he suffers a very paroxysm of agonized sincerity. It can last but a moment. The crisis passes, and the reaction follows. He takes refuge from himself in a wild orgy of reckless jesting:—"But see here, my friends! I forgot to tell you about my relics. Here they are—the best in England—and first-rate pardons, too! It's a regular insurance policy to have a Pardoner like me in the company. Come up, and make your offerings. You first, Sir Host! for I'm sure you are the worst sinner in the troop."

Harry Bailly has no conception (how could he?) of the Pardoner's emotional crisis. He answers with rough jocularity; but he means no offence, and, under ordinary circumstances the Pardoner would simply have paid him tit for tat. But the moment is too intense for poise. With another revulsion of feeling, the Pardoner becomes furiously angry, so angry that words stick in his throat.

> This Pardoner answerde nat a word;
> So wrooth he was, no word ne wolde he seye.
> "Now," quod oure Hoost, "I wol no lenger pleye
> With thee, ne with noon other angry man!"
>
>   (956–58)

"I won't joke," cries the Host indignantly, "with a man that cannot keep his temper."

Then the Knight interposes to make up the quarrel. They are reconciled amidst the laughter of the company. For nobody but Geoffrey Chaucer divined the tragic face behind the satyr's mask,—Geoffrey Chaucer, poet, idealist, burgher of London, Commissioner of Dykes and Ditches, who loved his fellow-men, both good and bad, and found no answer to the puzzle of life but in truth and courage and beauty and belief in God.

Germaine Dempster: from *Dramatic Irony in Chaucer*

In Chaucer's tale, the secondary ironic possibilities of the theme are completely sacrificed in favor of the one really tragic motif of the quest of Death. That the author of the *Merchant's* and the *Franklin's Tales* was capable of detecting and developing those secondary possibilities is obvious enough. We have to admit that he deliberately sacrificed all the contrasts that depended mostly on human actions and their consequences because he preferred to emphasize fully the one contrast in which Fate itself was seen at work. How did he make this the central feature of his story?

First of all, he realized that there was little contrast between a short and quite accidental quest of Death by companions who, one minute before, were ready for any adventure whatever—as is the case in all known analogues—and the fact that on that quest they actually meet their death. How much more tragic and intense if the three companions could be given a real reason why they should start on a mad and feverish, though consistent and deliberate, quest of Death! What associations of ideas brought the specific details of the tavern scene in Flanders during a pestilence it is impossible to ascertain. And it matters little here; the important point is the admirable skill with which Chaucer uses these new details to create the proper atmosphere, an atmosphere of heavy fear and sin, the mood of a *Danse macabre,* with the horror of Death increased by his mysterious character.

This background created, Chaucer tells us how his three "riotours" swear to find "this false traytour Deeth" and to kill him who has slain so many of their friends, and how they proceed on their way, sticking to their purpose in their obstinacy of rioters "al dronken":

> And many a grisly ooth thanne han they sworn,
> And Cristes blessed body al torente—
> "Deeth shal be deed, if that they may hym hente."
> (708–10)

The enigmatic character of the old man they meet on their way, the lines in which one of the revelers—perhaps not wrongly—accuses him of being the spy of Death, and the veiled challenge (or warning?) of the

From Dramatic Irony in Chaucer *by Germaine Dempster, Stanford University Publications: University Series: Language and Literature, Volume IV, Number 3 (Stanford: Stanford University Press, 1932; reprinted New York: The Humanities Press, 1959), pp. 77–79. Copyright 1932 by the Board of Trustees of the Leland Stanford Junior University. Reprinted by permission of The Humanities Press.*

old man—"Noght for youre boost he wole him no thyng hyde" (764)[1] (a
retort, perhaps, to the rioters' question, "Why artow al forwrapped
save thy face?") (718)—all this contributes to heighten the impression
and keep up the great "leitmotiv" Death.

The three revelers proceed till they come to that tree under which
the reader, just like the revelers themselves, half expects to find the
grim reaper with his scythe. He is accordingly quite prepared to identify
with Death whatever will be found under that tree. Here again we must
commend the skilful way in which Chaucer has kept us in suspense:
in all the other versions we know beforehand that the three companions are to find a heap of gold, and, if we are to notice the connection
between the short quest of Death, that heap of gold, and the end of
the story, we must be reminded now and then that there is such a connection. This is Hans Sachs's technique; it verges on artificiality; the
author's personality is distinctly perceived between the object and us.
But Chaucer has done enough by way of preparation and he knows
that we cannot miss the irony. One line more is enough, a line that
needs no commentary:

> No lenger thanne after Deeth they soughte.   (772)

They do not seek him any more; they do not even remember him. This
complete forgetfulness is infinitely more tragic than the mood of de-
fiant security of Sachs's robbers. They, at least, kept repeating that they
had not found Death after all, showing thereby that they were still
somewhat on their guard, that Fate could not have taken them entirely
by surprise.

Chaucer's revelers forget Death, but the reader does not. He is hurried through the last episodes without any secondary touch of dramatic
irony to distract his attention from the fulfillment of the grim proph-
ecy.[2] From that moment on, everything Chaucer says is a definite step
toward that fulfillment, and is felt as such. Fate, we know, is at work.

Fate or the Christian God? Though the *Pardoner's Tale* is a sermon,
there is room for doubt. We shall see later that the background of ac-

---

[1] There is another such veiled threat in ll. 744–47:

> I yeve yow reed,
> Ne dooth unto an oold man noon harm now,
> Namoore than ye wolde men did to yow
> In age, *if that ye so longe abyde.*

[2] In exactly ten lines (879–88) the one who has been sent for food is killed, the
other two sit down to their meal, drink the poisoned wine, and die. The irony of
their expectations is dismissed in two lines:

> Now lat us sitte and drynke, and make us merie,
> And afterward we wol his body berie.
>
> (883–84)

It could hardly be less.

cepted Christian faith is about the least favorable background possible for dramatic irony. The only form it allows is poetic justice, and that only as far as the punishment of the wicked goes. The irony of the *Pardoner's Tale* is obviously more than that. Punishing the revelers for their sins could be called poetic justice, but starting them on a deliberate quest for Death is creating a luxury of contrast to be enjoyed for its own sake, independently of moral values. Chaucer, the great dramatic artist, has emphasized the tragically ironic side of this story so much that he has overstepped a little, I fear, the bounds of classical sermon literature. The mysterious old man helps to carry us into a country of doubtful religious coloring.[3] We do not feel quite sure that the power behind the curtain is clearly and plainly the Christian God as chastiser of the wicked. Like Death in the tale, that power is impressive in proportion to its enigmatical character.

G. D. Josipovici: from "Fiction and Game in The Canterbury Tales"

The Pardoner's Prologue and Tale stands at the centre of *The Canterbury Tales*. It reveals the final turn of the ironic screw. Other tales had been told with another end in view than the winning of the prize dinner. The Miller had told a tale about a carpenter who aimed higher than was natural and so fell lower, and the Reeve had replied in similar vein with a story about a miller. The pilgrims could sit back and laugh at the knaves who fool others only to be fooled in their turn through lack of self-knowledge, and the reader could laugh with them. But the Pardoner has designs upon the whole company of pilgrims, and so, implicitly, upon ourselves, the readers.

What the Pardoner does is to tell the company that he is going to fool them, and then to go ahead and do it. As the pilgrims drink in the conclusion of the tale of the three rioters and submit to the inevitable moral:

> Now, goode men, God foryeve yow youre trespas,
> And ware yow fro the synne of avarice!
> Myn hooly pardoun may yow alle warice,
> So that ye offre nobles or sterlynges,
> Or elles silver broches, spoones, rynges.

> (904–8)

[3] The story is almost certainly of Eastern origin. See H. S. Canby, "Some Comments on the Sources of Chaucer's *Pardoner's Tale*," *Mod. Phil.*, II (1905), 477–87.

From "Fiction and Game in The Canterbury Tales" *by G. D. Josipovici, in* Critical Quarterly, *VII (1965), 193–197. Published by the Critical Quarterly Society. Reprinted by permission of the author.*

they automatically reach into their pockets, only to be brought up sharp by the sudden realisation that the Pardoner is only going through his old routine, which he had explained at length in his Prologue. The reaction of the Host is violent in the extreme:

> But, by the croys which that Seint Eleyne fond,
> I wolde I hadde thy coillons in myn hond
> In stide of relikes or of seintuarie.
>
> (951–53)

The Pardoner grows speechless with indignation at this, and a fight seems to be about to break out when the Knight interposes, reminding Harry Bailly of what he had himself so often said to cover up his own insults, that all this is nothing but a game:

> Namoore of this, for it is right ynough!
> Sire Pardoner, be glad and myrie of cheere;
> And ye, sire Hoost, that been to me so deere,
> I prey yow that ye kisse the Pardoner.
> And Pardoner, I prey thee, drawe thee neer,
> And, as we diden, lat us laughe and pleye.
>
> (962–67)

It would be a mistake to imagine that the Host is angry because the Pardoner has asked him for money. What arouses his indignation is that the Pardoner has fooled him. The Pardoner is not out to make money off the pilgrims, otherwise he would never have revealed to them so candidly his methods of doing so in his Prologue. What he is out for is to prove the power of his words, and in order to succeed he has to make the pilgrims see that he has been able to fool them despite their previous knowledge of his methods. In that moment between the conclusion of his tale and the outraged cry of the Host, the moment when the power of his rhetoric wears off enough to be recognised as such, he has won his victory. And as the power he is allowed to exercise over others under cover of the game seemed more important to the Host than the money he might make over the prize dinner, so we may be sure that the Pardoner would not have foregone his mental triumph for all the relics in the world.

But what in fact has the Pardoner done that was so obnoxious? After all, he has only played the game to its limits. His tale is the very reverse of that of the Parson, since it accepts itself as merely a tale. Although on the one level it is aimed at making a fool of everybody, on another level it is not aimed against anyone—except those who refuse to recognise it as a fiction, a tale told as part of a game.

The Pardoner, however, has fared ill at the hands of modern critics. In a brilliant article Robert P. Miller has summed up the current attitude towards him:

. . . the *Pardoner's Tale* fits generally into a scheme of opposition between Charity and Cupidity in *The Canterbury Tales* as a whole. The extreme maliciousness of the Pardoner as a person sets him at the far end of the scale among the pilgrims. As a type he is even more definitely evil. He is the false eunuch who stands and points the way up the wrong road. He represents the way of cupidity, malice, impenitence, spiritual sterility—just the opposite of the way of the Parson and his spiritual brother, the Plowman. He is that Old Man as he lives and exerts his influence in the great pilgrimage of life. And as the *vetus homo* he is to be opposed to the Christlike figure of the *novus homo,* the true guide—the "povre Persoun of a toun." [1]

In the way it brings together the figure of the Pardoner as he is described in the *General Prologue,* and the themes of the Pardoner's own prologue and tale, Miller's article is exemplary. Miller does, however, forget one crucial fact: that the Pardoner is a fictional creation of the poet Chaucer, and that we are misreading the poem if we apply the same criteria in judging him as we would a real person. St. Augustine, whose theology lies behind Miller's analysis, knew better when, in his *Soliloquia,* discussing the nature of artistic illusion, he said:

> For how could he whom I have mentioned [the actor Roscius] have been a true tragedian, had he been unwilling to be a false Hector, a false Andromache, a false Hercules, and innumerable other things? or how would a picture, for instance, be a true picture, unless it were a false horse? . . . Wherefore, if it avails some things that they be somewhat false in order that they may be somewhat true; why do we so greatly dread falsity, and seek truth as the greatest good? [2]

Miller reads *The Pardoner's Tale* in more or less the same way as does Harry Bailly: as a personal affront which can only be met by showing up the evil of the teller. But the tale was only told in play, and the right reaction is the Knight's: to accept the joke and learn from it. There is perhaps some excuse for the Host; his reaction is the kind that one makes in everyday life to the realisation that one has been fooled. Although ostensibly part of the game instigated by Harry Bailly himself, it is not too difficult to see that the Pardoner's tale is not quite as disinterested as his fulfilling of the rules might imply. The pleasure he takes in fooling the pilgrims through the power of his words is probably more loathsome, because cleverer, than Harry Bailly's sneering bonhomie. For the reader of Chaucer, however, to re-act in this way is to misunderstand the whole nature of Chaucer's irony. For if the reaction of the Host is similar to that which one makes in everyday

---

[1] Robert P. Miller, "Chaucer's Pardoner, the Scriptural Eunuch, and the *Pardoner's Tale,*" *Speculum,* XXX (1955), 198–99. [Reprinted here, see pp. 43–69 —ED.]

[2] Quoted in Singleton, *Dante Studies I,* Harvard University Press, 1954, pp. 63–64.

life, the reaction of the Knight is of the kind that games try to foster, and which an ironic art like Chaucer's or Sterne's tries to produce.

The Pardoner's Prologue and Tale stands at the centre of *The Canterbury Tales* because it is a paradigm of the whole poem. All the tales, and the poem as a whole, can be seen as an effort to bring to the consciousness of the reader the fact that it is easier to lay down rules for others than to abide by them oneself, easier to invoke the game when it is oneself who is making the jokes than when one is the victim of a joke. This is the theme of the tales of the Miller, the Reeve, the Merchant, and the Nun's Priest. But it is also the theme of the debate between the Miller and the Reeve, the Friar and the Summoner. The Miller is as blind to the mote in his own eye as is John the Carpenter, the gull of his tale. But the Reeve, who points this out to him, and goes on to tell a tale of a gulled miller, is equally blind. All the pilgrims and the characters in their tales are quite capable of seeing the folly of others, but none is capable of seeing that he too is tainted. And the regression from John the Carpenter to the Miller to the Reeve can end only with one person: the reader. After he has laughed with the Miller at John, and with Chaucer and the Reeve at the Miller, and with Chaucer at the Reeve, the reader suddenly finds, as the Host found at the close of the Pardoner's tale, that the joke is on himself. And at this point there is only one way of escape: to acknowledge one's folly and learn from the game. The Pardoner's ironic self-revelation is a mirror of Chaucer's insistence that his poem is not truth but fiction.

Nancy H. Owen: from "The Pardoner's Introduction, Prologue and Tale"

The sermon comprises lines 329–918, which I should divide, according to medieval homiletic classification, in the following way:

329–34   theme
335–422 protheme
423–26   restatement of theme
427–62   introduction of theme
463–660 process and development of principals
661–894 major *exemplum*
895–915 conclusion
916–18   benediction

From "The Pardoner's Introduction, Prologue and Tale: Sermon and Fabliau" by Nancy H. Owen, in the Journal of English and Germanic Philology, *LXVI* (*1967*), 543–47. Copyright © *1967 by the Board of Trustees of the University of Illinois. Reprinted by permission of the University of Illinois Press.*

In the theme, and indeed in the protheme, restatement of theme, and introduction of theme, the Pardoner fuses revelation of his homiletic technique with the normal requirements of each of these sermon parts. Having introduced his text, *"Radix malorum est Cupiditas"* (I Tim. 6:10), with the explanation that, according to his habitual practice in preaching, his "theme is alwey oon, and evere was" (333), he passes into the protheme (335–422), the introductory prelocution which may include an illustration of the text. The Pardoner's methods of getting money by means of his preaching and selling of relics provide an illustration of his text. This protheme leads most naturally into the restatement of his theme:

> But shortly myn entente I wol devyse:
> I preche of no thyng but for coveityse.
> Therfore my theme is yet, and evere was,
> *Radix malorum est Cupiditas.*   (423–26)

Now he turns to that part, the introduction of the theme (427–62), which is intended to make his purpose clear. And he does make his purpose abundantly clear: to turn his audience from avarice in order that their money may line his pocket.

> Thus kan I preche agayn that same vice
> Which that I use, and that is avarice.
> But though myself be gilty in that synne,
> Yet kan I maken oother folk to twynne
> From avarice, and soore to repente.
> But that is nat my principal entente;
> I preche nothyng but for coveitise.
>
>   (427–33)

He concludes this statement of purpose as boldly as he began it: "A moral tale yet I yow telle kan,/ Which I am wont to preche for to wynne" (460–61).

The process, which includes, the plan or scheme of the sermon, its divisions or principals, should be next. Here, however, Chaucer brilliantly fuses narrative technique with homiletic structure. The Pardoner begins his tale, or major *exemplum*, "In Flaundres whilom was a compaignye" (463), but quickly the tale merges into the process, fuses with it (465–76), recedes before the entrance into the tavern of dancers, fruit venders, confectioners, singers, and whores (477–82), and disappears completely after line 482. . . .

There follows, completing the process, a series of three *exempla* taken from Scripture which illustrate drunkenness, as an offspring of gluttony and as a parent of lechery. These brief asides are intruded here, apart from their connection to one of his principals—gluttony— but also, one supposes, as ironic comments on the Pardoner's earlier line, "Now have I dronke a draughte of corny ale" (456), and on his recognized sexual deficiency.

Next, the three principals—gluttony, gaming, and swearing—are each treated separately, each subdivided as needed, and each illustrated through *exempla*. Gluttony is subdivided into two parts—overeating and overdrinking—and each part is exemplified (498–588). Gaming or hazardry is defined and twice illustrated (589–628). Swearing is subdivided into great swearing and false swearing, and each illustrated (629–59). The Pardoner turns from his illustration of these sins of the tavern to the tale itself, to the three rioters sitting in the tavern. The tale is a lengthy *exemplum* (661–894) illustrating how avarice, compounded by greed for food and drink, by false and great swearing, and by playing games of chance, can lead men to murder and to spiritual death.

Having amply illustrated his theme, he plunges into his conclusion or final peroration (895–915). He scores all the sins he has so effectively pictured in process, principals, and *exemplum:*

> O cursed synne of alle cursednesse!
> O traytours homycide, O wikkednesse!
> O glotonye, luxurie, and hasardrye!
> Thou blasphemour of Crist with vileynye
> And othes grete, of usage and of pride!
>
> . . . .
>
> Now, goode men, God foryeve yow youre trespas,
> And ware yow fro the synne of avarice!
>
> (895–99, 904–5)

Then he offers the services of his powers of absolution and pardon and ends his sermon, "And lo, sires, thus I preche" (915). Yet it is not quite the end, because he concludes with a benediction:

> And Jhesu Crist, that is oure soules leche,
> So graunte yow his pardoun to receyve,
> For that is best; I wol yow nat deceyve.
>
> (916–18)

This benediction is a final example of the Pardoner's extraordinary honesty toward the pilgrims. He does not swerve from this honesty until, as a last joke, he offers them his false relics and pardons, which they know to be fraudulent. Then they can no longer tolerate him and turn against him,[1] in the person of the Host, to whom the Pardoner directs the first invitation to kiss the false relics. The Host retorts in kind:

[1] Their revulsion against him was suggested in the "Introduction," 323–26.

> "Nay, nay!" quod he, "thanne have I Cristes curs!
> Lat be," quod he, "it shal nat be, so theech!
> Thou woldest make me kisse thyn olde breech,
> And swere it were a relyk of a seint,
> Though it were with thy fundement depeint!
> But, by the croys which that Seint Eleyne fond,
> I wolde I hadde thy coillons in myn hond
> In stide of relikes or of seintuarie.
> Lat kutte hem of, I wol thee helpe hem carie;
> They shul be shryned in an hogges toord!"
>
> (946–55)

The change in mood from an honest benediction to the lowest tom-foolery is as abrupt as the earlier change from the Host's demand for merriment which was clamorously voted down by the pilgrims in favor of "som moral thyng." In other words, we are thrust into the sermon and thrust out of it as well.

Rosemond Tuve: from *Allegorical Imagery*

[Miss Tuve has been discussing the feminine personifications of the Seven Deadly Sins in Guillaume de Deguileville's *Pelerinage de la vie humaine*—ED.] To the three pages opening out the traits of Pride before she declares herself, there are added seven after that, powerful with that tone of exultant revelation which each ancient evil exhibits as soon as she has said her name. Envy tastes and savors the fear of others at her basilisk's eyes. Detraction, Envy's daughter, gloats and rejoices that she has a throat bloody as a wolf that has just strangled a sheep in the fold, "I am of the lynage of the raven that hath mad his nest in hell. I love to eat caraynes"—the more stinkinge the better, for rottenness is her life and her nurture. . . . Frequently the long recitals are packed with very precise things "I" (Ire, Gluttony, Lechery) do or have done. What is so characteristically allegorical about these figures is not the element of an abstraction personified, doing actions, but the fact that the suffocating, piled-up concretions define and realize a universal that has a life and a nature of its own.

These unabashed self-revelations convey pure evil with a mounting intensity which is shocking, even terrifying if we feel self-convicted, an effect something like that of James's *Beast in the Jungle.* The methods are not as different as they seem, for the secret of this power—more

From Allegorical Imagery: Some Medieval Books and Their Posterity *by Rose-mond Tuve (Princeton: Princeton University Press, 1966), pp. 176–77. Copyright © 1966 by Princeton University Press. Reprinted by permission of the publisher.*

overt in allegorical writing—is its accepted right to abstract and present the very thing-in-itself. This cannot be conveyed by selective quotation; the hag Envy and her terrible daughters, and Avarice, are particularly fearful. Could I present the latter, readers too might share
my suspicion that there is a relation here with the self-revelations of
Chaucer's Pardoner. The blatant and exultant tone which has always
been an embarrassment in explanations that stress some psychological
"situation-al" cause (like Kittredge's) is completely proper if we are
viewing the very essence of Covetousness in a human form. He shares
an unmistakable ecstatic timbre with all those characters who "present"
an evil in Guillaume and parts of the *Roman de la rose*. This is the
only tale of Chaucer's that is truly hospitable to such interpretations
(witness the Old Man), though in others there is a good deal of simpler
moral "signification." More figurative meanings do not here militate
against our appreciation of his creation of full, living, complicated
human characters (a different thing but no more literary).

D. W. Robertson, Jr.: from *A Preface to Chaucer*

The pardoner is not only cupidinous himself; he deliberately fosters
cupidity in his audience while developing the theme *radix malorum
est cupiditas*. He tempts his listeners by assuring them that the proper
application of his "relics" will multiply the "beestes" and the "stoor"
of his customers, cause them to be unconcerned about the marital in-
fidelities of their spouses, and bring about a "multiplying" of grain.
In other words, he appeals to their cupidity and encourages it, at the
same time seeking to satisfy his own. He tells entertaining stories so
that his words will be more profitable to himself in a material way, but
these stories, he assures us, can be moral. And he proceeds to tell a
moral story in the development of his theme which actually constitutes
a kind of self-portrait. From an exegetical point of view, the expository
development which the pardoner applies to his theme is vivid, energetic, and not without subtlety. He subdivides *cupiditas* into three
parts: gluttony, gambling, and swearing. The first leads to the death
of the spirit (cf. 1 Tim. 5: 6):

> he that haunteth swiche delices
> Is deed, whil that he lyveth in tho vices.

The second is the "mooder of lesynges," and the third is a violation
of the Second Commandment (640–42). In the sermon itself, these trans-

gressions are not ordered in accordance with any set principles, or at least the principles are not made explicit, probably because Chaucer did not wish the pardoner to seem aware of the implications of what he says for himself. The three sins may, however, be seen as a progression along the road to spiritual death: (1) the submission of the spirit to the flesh in gluttony, foreshadowed, as the pardoner suggests, by the sin of Adam and Eve, (2) the submission to Fortune implied by gambling, and (3) the denial of Christ, which is the "spiritual" implication of violating the Second Commandment. Hence, the three sins reflect the old pattern of the temptations of the flesh, the world, and the Devil, for submission to Fortune is submission to the world, and the denial of Christ is the ultimate aim of the Devil's temptation. All men seek to conquer death, to find, in one way or another, a death for death. For Christians the road to this achievement was foreseen by the prophet Osee [13: 14]: "O death, I will be thy death." As St. Paul explains it [1 Cor. 15: 53ff.], "this corruptible must put on incorruption; and this mortal must put on immortality. And when this mortal hath put on immortality, then shall come to pass the saying that is written: 'Death is swallowed up in victory. O death, where is thy victory? O death, where is thy sting?' Now the sting of death is sin: and the power of sin is the law."

Death may be conquered, that is, through the New Man. But there are also those who seek the same goal through the pardoner's three sins. Having allowed the flesh to dominate the spirit, or, in Pauline language, having given themselves up to the counsels of the Old Man, they seek satisfaction in the realm of Fortune and become members of that sect whose "wombe is hir god" and who are "enemys of Cristes croys" [Phil. 3: 18ff.]. But this pursuit leads only to death rather than to the death of death. The rioters of the pardoner's exemplum give themselves up to gluttony in drunkenness, seek the counsel of the Old Man, immerse themselves in a lust for worldly treasure, and, finally, deny the bond of sworn brotherhood which unites them as each makes himself the object of his worship. But the pardoner has given himself up wholeheartedly to the same pursuit. He will do anything to satisfy his flesh, he abuses the Word of God for worldly ends, and he ends his sermon by first calling attention to Christ's pardon and then denying it by offering his wares to the pilgrims. Taken as a whole, the Pardoner's Tale is an excellent illustration of what happens to those who deny the spirit of Christ beneath the letter of the text *radix malorum est cupiditas* and devote themselves to the pursuit of the corporal rather than the intelligible. Their pursuit ends in the denial of the spirit everywhere, and it would be difficult to imagine a more forceful and vivid denunciation of this denial than that which Chaucer has left us in the pardoner's prologue and tale.

Chronology of Important Dates

Chaucer	The Age
1215	Pope Innocent III promulgates first general code for control of pardoners.
1232	Earl of Pembroke deeds property at Charing to Order of St. Mary Roncevall.
1300	Pope Boniface VIII's Jubilee Year.
*ca.*1313	Dante (d. 1321) completes the *Commedia*.
1337	Hundred Years' War with France begins.
1343–44 Chaucer born.	
1348–49	First outbreak of Black Death (repeated outbreaks in 1361–62 and 1369).
1362	Formal establishment of English as official language: Parliament first opened in English; Statute of Pleading.
1369	*Book of the Duchess* composed.
1372 Chaucer's first Italian journey (second in 1378).	
1377	Death of Edward III; accession of Richard II.
1378	Great Schism: rival popes at Rome and Avignon.
1381	Peasants' Revolt.
1385–90 Chaucer's Italian "translations": *Troilus and Criseyde,* "Knight's Tale," "Clerk's Tale."	
1390–1400 Chaucer composes most of the *Canterbury Tales,* including the "Pardoner's Tale."	St. Mary Roncevall's building-fund drive for the hospital at Charing.
1399	Henry Bolingbroke (Henry IV) deposes Richard II; Chaucer retires to grounds of Westminster Abbey.
1400 Chaucer dies.	

Notes on the Editor and Contributors

DEWEY R. FAULKNER is Assistant Professor of English at Yale University, where he teaches the medieval and romantic periods.

JANET ADELMAN is Associate Professor of English at the University of California, Berkeley. She is the author of *The Common Liar: An Essay on "Antony and Cleopatra."*

STEPHEN A. BARNEY is Assistant Professor of English at Yale University. He has published essays on Chaucer and Langland.

BERTRAND H. BRONSON has retired from the University of California, Berkeley. He is especially noted for his books and essays on Chaucer, on Dr. Johnson, and on the ballad.

GERMAINE DEMPSTER taught at the University of Chicago. Author of numerous essays on Chaucerian texts, sources, and other matters, she is best known as coeditor of *Sources and Analogues of Chaucer's "Canterbury Tales."*

RALPH W. V. ELLIOTT is Professor of English in the Flinders University of South Australia. He is the author of *Runes: An Introduction,* a commentary on the *General Prologue,* and essays on various medieval and modern works.

DAVID V. HARRINGTON is Professor of English at Gustavus Adolphus College. He has published essays on Chaucer and medieval and modern literature.

GABRIEL D. JOSIPOVICI teaches at the University of Sussex. He is the author of *The World and the Book* and of essays on a wide variety of topics and is also a novelist and playwright.

GEORGE LYMAN KITTREDGE taught for many years at Harvard University and is justly famous as editor of Shakespeare and as author of works on Chaucer, on ballads, on philology, and on many other subjects.

ROBERT P. MILLER is Associate Professor of English at Queens College of the City University of New York. He has published other essays on Chaucer besides the well-known one reprinted in this selection.

NANCY H. OWEN teaches at the Northview School in Pasadena. She has published articles on medieval literature.

D. W. ROBERTSON, JR. is Professor of English at Princeton University. Among his numerous books and essays are *A Preface to Chaucer* and *Chaucer's London;* he has edited *The Literature of Medieval England.*

JOHN M. STEADMAN is Professor of English at the University of California, Riverside, and Senior Research Associate at the Huntington Library. Well-known for his work in the Renaissance and on Milton, he has recently published *Disembodied Laughter,* on Chaucer's *Troilus.*

ROSEMOND TUVE was Professor of English at Connecticut College. She is the author of *Allegorical Imagery, Elizabethan and Metaphysical Imagery,* and of essays on Spenser, Herbert, and Milton.

Selected Bibliography

On the Pardoner himself, see Muriel Bowden, *A Commentary on the General Prologue to the Canterbury Tales*, 2nd ed. (New York: The Macmillan Company, 1967), pp. 274–90; and Walter Clyde Curry, "The Pardoner's Secret" in *Chaucer and the Medieval Sciences*, rev. ed. (New York: Barnes and Noble, 1960), pp. 54–70. The historical background of pardoners is given most fully in Alfred L. Kellogg and Louis A. Haselmayer, "Chaucer's Satire of the Pardoner," *PMLA*, LXVI (1951), pp. 251–77; this has been reprinted in Alfred L. Kellogg, *Chaucer, Langland, Arthur: Essays in Middle English Literature* (New Brunswick, N. J.: Rutgers University Press, 1972), pp. 212–44. Of general assistance are the extensive and very useful introduction and notes in *The Pardoner's Prologue and Tale*, ed. A. C. Spearing (Cambridge: Cambridge University Press, 1965); also helpful is the commentary in *Chaucer's Poetry*, ed. E. T. Donaldson (New York: Ronald Press, 1958), pp. 927–30. The remainder of R. W. V. Elliott's essay in *The Nun's Priest's Tale and The Pardoner's Tale* (Oxford: Basil Blackwell, 1965) is recommended.

Useful summaries of criticism, each with its own synthesizing interpretation, are the following: G. G. Sedgewick, "The Progress of Chaucer's Pardoner, 1880–1940," *Modern Language Quarterly*, I (1940), pp. 431–58; [reprinted in both *Chaucer: Modern Essays in Criticism*, ed. Edward Wagenknecht (New York: Oxford University Press, 1959), pp. 126–58, and *Chaucer Criticism: The Canterbury Tales*, ed. Richard J. Schoeck and Jerome Taylor (Notre Dame: University of Notre Dame Press, 1960), pp. 190–220]; Paull F. Baum, "Chaucer and the Scholars: The Pardoner" in *Chaucer: A Critical Appreciation* (Durham, N. C.: Duke University Press, 1958), pp. 44–59; and John Halverson, "Chaucer's Pardoner and the Progress of Criticism," *Chaucer Review*, IV (1970), 184–202.

A reading of the tale from the "Robertsonian" point of view is in Bernard F. Huppé's *A Reading of the Canterbury Tales*, rev. ed. (Albany: State University of New York Press, 1967), pp. 209–220. The relation of the Pardoner to one of his literary ancestors, Faux-Semblant in the *Romance of the Rose*, is discussed in P. M. Kean, *Chaucer and the Making of English Poetry, Volume II: The Art of Narrative* (London and Boston: Routledge and Kegan Paul, 1972), pp. 96–109. The ending of the poem is discussed in two recent studies: Charles Muscatine, *Poetry and Crisis in the Age of Chaucer* (Notre Dame and London: University of Notre Dame Press, 1972), pp. 116–18; and Norman E. Eliason, *The Language of Chaucer's Poetry: An Appraisal of the Verse, Style, and Structure*, Anglistica, Vol. XVII (Copenhagen: Rosenkilde and Bagger, 1972), pp. 201–6.

Information on how Chaucer's contemporaries read the tale aloud can be found in Ian Robinson's *Chaucer's Prosody* (Cambridge: Cambridge University Press, 1971), especially pp. 162–64. The earliest known illustrations to the tale, carved on an elm chest-front dated *ca.*1400, have recently been first exhibited; a photograph is included in the exhibition catalogue by Brian Spencer, *Chaucer's London* (London: Her Majesty's Stationery Office, for the London Museum, 1972), ill. 34. (This extraordinarily interesting booklet can be obtained from The London Museum, Kensington Palace, London W8 4PX.) It has also been reproduced with Sally Paine Kington's review of the exhibition in *The Connoisseur* (April 1972), p. 302.